D0848056

Love Leaves No Choice

Life-style Evangelism

Love Leaves No Choice

Life-style Evangelism

~~~~~~~~~~~~~~~~~~~~~~~~~~~~~~~~~~~~~

C. B. Hogue

Word Books, Publisher
Waco, Texas

LOVE LEAVES NO CHOICE

ISBN # 0–87680–471–7
Library of Congress catalog card number: 76–5720

NOV 19, 1976

To
my wife
Betty Jane

Contents

Foreword 9
Preface 11
1. A Gauntlet Cast 13
2. The Primacy of Evangelism 25
3. Inevitable Evangelism 35
4. Evangelism—the Spark and the Fire 47
5. God's Liberation Movement 61
6. Evangelism, Youth, and Change 73
7. Evangelism—Proclamation to the Masses 83
8. Evangelism and Disciple-making 97
9. Evangelism—Overwhelmed by Opinions 107
10. Innovations and Change 119
11. Equipped to Evangelize 131
12. Life-style Evangelism 147
Epilogue 157
Bibliography 160

Foreword

This book by Dr. C. B. Hogue is unique. As its message unfolds you will be led to several profitable conclusions. Some of these conclusions we have heard of and sometimes acted upon. But in this book a climax is reached in what the author has delineated as "life-style evangelism." This describes evangelism as a natural expression of discipleship and this is what evangelism should be. It must be natural. Too long we have allowed ourselves to be preoccupied with method and technique in our attempt to fulfill the commission of our Lord. Dr. Hogue is calling us back to these basic qualities of our faith that will commend Jesus to a world in need. Dr. Hogue has suggested some things to do to evangelize effectively. But he has put the emphasis where it belongs—upon what we should *be* in our relationship to both our Lord and our fellowman. I urge you to read it and to read it all the way through.

BILLY GRAHAM

Preface

I am sharing this book with you because I have a conviction that God has commissioned us to evangelize our world. "The love of Christ leaves us no choice" (2 Cor. 5:14, NEB). The immensity of this task may appear staggering and its responsibilities overwhelming, *but we really have no choice.* I have tried to take you with me on my journey in this book. I think I can say with John "We have heard it; we have seen it with our own eyes; we looked upon it; and felt it with our own hands; and it is of this we tell. Our theme is the word of life. This life was made visible; we have seen it and bear our testimony" (1 John 1:1–2, NEB). I am not alone on this journey. All around me there are, thank God, "a cloud of witnesses." May God help us to see them and know that they are always there.

C. B. HOGUE
Atlanta, Georgia

1

A
Gauntlet Cast

The hand of the Lord was upon me, and He brought me out by
the Spirit of the Lord and set me down in the middle of the
valley; and it was full of bones. And He caused me to pass among
them round about, and behold, there were very many on the
surface of the valley; and lo, they were very dry. And He said to
me, "Son of man, can these bones live?" And I answered,
"O Lord God, Thou knowest." And He said to me, "Prophesy
over these bones, and say to them 'O dry bones, hear the word of
the Lord.' " Thus says the Lord God to these bones, "Behold,
I will cause breath to enter you that you may come to life"
(Ezek. 37:1–5).

1

Prologue

As I watched the hands of the World Population Clock inexorably, relentlessly ticking off each moment's births, a chilling feeling of powerlessness and hopelessness tinged with awe swept over me.

The implications were staggering.

With each slow, steady click of those giant hands, our already overcrowded, undernourished world added one hundred people; each sweep across the clock's face meant 144,000 new human beings had boarded planet earth. In the United States alone, the population was growing by six persons a minute, 360 persons an hour, 8,600 persons a day, 60,000 persons a week.

The frightening reality was that world-wide, before I could walk across the foyer and into the auditorium where a speaker was calling the 4,000 delegates to the World Evangelism Conference to "let the earth hear God's voice," several hundred people would be born who would, in all likelihood, never hear of God or of the hope embodied in the life of God's Son, Jesus of Nazareth.

And I wondered, there in that hall in Lausanne, Switzerland, "God, does it have to be . . . ?"

1

A
Gauntlet Cast

This book is my plea—and, perhaps, my demand—that Christians not let it be . . . if you please, *a gauntlet cast*.

Christians must hear the human voices behind these numbers; they must become concerned enough to recognize the personal challenge of these faceless masses; they must, in short, accept the responsibility inherent in discipleship.

The enormity of the task confronting Christ's followers can shatter the senses. Consider just the United States: Of the 210 plus million people who live here now, only 40 percent of them—approximately 84 million people—attend any kind of religious service during a given week. Over half of the population has not attended any religious service in the past 30 days; one-third of the population does not even claim any religious affiliation. And those percentages increase daily!

Our "one nation under God" writhes with the instability of a citizenry without an established standard of conduct, without a clear and universal moral code. Life-style, dress, diet, employment, recreation, and leisure activities all reflect a society in flux.

Our people live in a traumatic state of change, shaken by war, political and social scandal, inflation, sexism, recession, drugs, and alcohol. They are satiated by affluence and bored by materialism. Amidst perversions such as the occult, sexual excesses, satan worship, they search for meaning.

And they come up empty.

Peace, security, love, hope—the sense of purpose they seek —are not commodities that can be purchased with dollars or earned by experiments with the latest fad. They are qualities given freely to those who have answered the ringing call for an authentic, life-changing conversion to Jesus Christ.

But Jesus' assurances are not one's protected property; they belong to all humans who would hear and accept the joy and promise of the Christ-life. The problem confronting the world today is that Christians fail so miserably to give people the chance to hear. They refuse to live the radical, dynamic evangelism that our times demand. There is an old saying that "if you keep your head while everyone around you is losing theirs, perhaps you don't understand the situation." If Christians fail to recognize the urgency of the hour, it is because they do not understand the consequences of their failure to act; they lack a sense of commitment based on their awareness of God's command.

God's plan for every person and every fellowship of believers is that they, individually and collectively, physically and verbally, present the Good News. In other words, they are to think and act evangelistically. But many Christians today react negatively to suggestions that they commit themselves totally to God's purposes.

Several factors are at play here.

First, common misconception labels "evangelism" as emotionalism. Those who view it this way fear the pulsation of the Holy Spirit and the demands the Spirit's gifts make on a renewed congregation and individual. They have a tendency to water down evangelism so that it includes everything done by the church rather than confining it to the confrontation of lost men with the Good News. Their "evangelism" is not the central distinctive of biblical concepts.

Second, God's teachings tell us there is a hell, an eternal separation from God, and that human beings who reject Jesus suffer this hell. Christians who refuse to proclaim Christ are either unconvinced of hell's reality or they are callous and unthinking. Certainly they exhibit little concern or compassion for others.

Others hide behind another smoke screen. They hesitate to confront someone with the demands of Christ because of cultural influences. We live under the basic philosophical presupposition of Western individualism that each man is his own keeper; Christians have no more right, says a philosophy, to infringe on the mental territorial space of others than do others —Buddhists or Moslems, for example—have the right to invade the Christian's mindset.

Third, their concern for others has been dulled or supplanted by other church emphases. In ecclesiastical history, whenever this has happened, church growth has waned.

Traditionally, without a focused zeal for leading lost souls to Christ, the fellowship of reconciliation has lost its power. Too much effort has been channeled into the forms of religion —too little on the practice of religion. The spring in the step of the believing Christian drags, the thrill of personal devotion dies; silence replaces the shout of the soul, emptiness stills the joy of sacrifice.

The church falls into complacency, characterized by mediocrity.

Evidence also indicates this fall comes when the fellowship of believers has run hither and yon at every whimper of discontent and criticism of the world. When the church becomes busy wiping noses, changing diapers, and goose-stepping to the world's commands, it loses sight of its absolute priority—the dissemination of the Good News of Jesus Christ. Says Michael

Green, principal of the London Divinity School, "Today much Christian life-style is indistinguishable from that of non-Christians, and much church fellowship is conspicuous for its coolness."

Obviously, rather than converting the world through bringing the lost to a knowledge of Jesus, Christians have been converted by the world to its own way of life.

Most people today are unaware of the Good News primarily because they have received no clear invitation from the body of believers to hear and rejoice in its hope.

This does not mean they haven't heard of Christ or Christianity; it is quite possible that many people in the world—and especially in the United States—*have* heard. But they do not understand. They have heard of Jesus and even use his name, but have not heard and believed his Good News! For some it is because they are members of special socio-economic or ethnic groups outside the normal perimeters of white Anglo-Saxon Protestant Christian outreach; for others it is because Christians insist on speaking the "language of Zion," as one Christian leader puts it, to people who don't identify with or hold in common the meaning of their terms. In either case, it is a clear indictment of selectivity in the presentation of Christ's message of hope and of life; both challenge us to a new thrust of dynamic evangelism.

A recent analysis of today's churches shows the average congregation is better equipped to handle every other task than it is to accomplish its primary responsibility of proclaiming the gospel of Christ. The church in America has good buildings, up-to-date equipment, well-prepared teaching materials and literature. Yet the emphasis is not on witnessing.. Look at your own church. In a court of law, could you find enough evidence to convict it of being an evangelistic center?

Billy Graham warns, "No matter how zealous or dedicated the Christian community, it is always in danger of having the vital nerve of evangelism cut from within. It can take place, for example, when Christians are conformed to the ease of this world, and they lose the urgency of the gospel message. It also happens when they become diverted into secondary issues and thus become preoccupied with things other than true evangelism."

The need today is for evangelism, dynamic evangelism, to become a ground swell; and for the people of the church, unashamed, bold, articulate, to recover the evangelistic thrust of the first-century Christians and embark afresh on a twentieth-century mission.

According to Michael Green, "When a movement grows from a dozen peasants in an unimportant corner of the world to the official religion of the civilized world inside 300 years; when it is sufficiently independent of that civilization since; when it is universal enough in its appeal to win millions of converts in all sectors of the globe among all types of men belonging to every culture and personality type—then it is arguable that such a movement has got something. It is arguable that we have a good deal to learn from its strategy and tactics, its methods and approaches."

The New Testament model is still possible, but not if we are uncertain of our responsibility; we have an example of dynamic evangelism that far exceeds our present lip service. "And they, continuing daily with one accord in the temple, and breaking bread from house to house, did eat their meat with gladness and singleness of heart, praising God, and having favour with all the people. And the Lord added to the church daily such as should be saved" (Acts 2:46–47, KJV). Never did the early Christians bog down in form or function; those early believers used every opportunity and every means available to spread the gospel. And they produced a dynamic evangelism unmatched in the history of Christianity. Evangelist Leslie Woodson defines evangelism as "the mission to bringing individuals into a personal confrontation with Jesus Christ and his demands upon their lives. It is challenging men to accept the highest level of living known to human beings, the dynamic and wholesome life of redemption and redemptiveness until all persons shall be witnesses to all other persons."

This was the spirit of the New Testament Christians; this is the mandate and model God commands for today. Such marching orders should not be confused with minor concerns which the average congregation has and which are sometimes twisted into perfunctory priorities. The redeemed fellowship of believers must concentrate now, as then, on the redemptive object of Christ's commission to make disciples, to evangelize the unevangelized.

Dynamic evangelism discovers that witness is the axis around which the total life of the church revolves. It is substance, commitment, proclamation; doing as well as believing. The Scriptures tell us, "By their fruits ye shall know them." Dynamic evangelism is that evangelistic style of life that encompasses all daily situations and experiences; it is total commitment to Christ and to the Christ-character way of life—an outlook on being that shares Christ freely, naturally, without prepackaging or ecclesiastically computerized programing.

Dynamic evangelism makes individuals so turned on to Jesus Christ that they want to share with everyone, everywhere, what he's done in their lives; there is no way to sound it in the wrong place. Its patterns and methods may vary, but its direction and goals remain constant and sufficient to reach the world for Christ. Flexible and adaptable, it is all things to all persons, yet it never compromises biblical perspective and truth.

Dynamic evangelism spans the years and seasons. It is a life-living, life-sharing existence. The commitment to Christ so controls the individual's day-to-day relationships that when an opportunity arises, he willingly proclaims the Good News he's found in Jesus Christ who is the heart and soul of all that we are and all that we do, who died for the sins of all and was raised from death by the Father, who offers to each person who responds to him the forgiveness of sins and the gift of the Holy Spirit.

"It seems to me high time we get evangelizing out of the theological basement," says author Seward Hiltner in *Ferment in Ministry*. "If we have a treasure to be shared with all men who will receive it, then let us get on with it."

The gauntlet has been cast before us; now is the time to pick it up and confront the world. I ask you, "Do we have a choice?"

2

The Primacy of Evangelism

Beware lest you forget the Lord your God by not keeping His commandments and His ordinances and His statutes which I am commanding you today; lest, when you have eaten and are satisfied, and have built good houses and lived in them, and when your herds and your flocks multiply, and your silver and gold multiply, and all that you have multiplies, then your heart becomes proud, and you forget the Lord your God who brought you out from the land of Egypt, out of the house of slavery. He led you through the great and terrible wilderness, with its fiery serpents and scorpions and thirsty ground where there was no water; He brought water for you out of the rock of flint. In the wilderness He fed you manna which your fathers did not know, that he might test you, to do good for you in the end. Otherwise, you may say in your heart, "My power and the strength of my hands made me this wealth." But you shall remember the Lord your God, for it is He who is giving you power to make wealth (Deut. 8:11–18a).

2

Prologue

I was a child of the Depression, youngest son of a tenant farmer who eked out a living on 160 acres of sandy ground near Stanton, Texas.

Besides myself, only one of my seven brothers graduated from high school; I am the only one to graduate from college.

My parents were Southern Baptists, but did not go to church when I was young. One of my brothers had polio; the experience unsettled my family. It appeared we wanted nothing to do with religion or God.

A pastor near us became concerned about our family; over a period of about two years, he got us back to church. I was nine or ten years old.

It was during a revival that I became a Christian. The preacher was holding open-air services on the side lawn of the church. He wasn't a great preacher, but his message had a hold on me. I was uneasy every time he gave the invitation for new believers to come forward and join the church. When my friends became Christians, I was moved.

During one service he said, "You can become a Christian anywhere if you will ask Christ to come into your heart."

I decided to try. One afternoon, when I was alone, I prayed. Nothing happened.

I went to church again that night; again I came under the conviction I had to do something about my life.

I knew the next time I was alone, I was going to have a problem. I dreaded it.

The next day, going out after the cows, I really got down to business with God. I asked him to come into my life. He did.

A year after that I joined the church. But there was no doubt my conversion came that afternoon. I didn't understand all of what happened to me because I hadn't been to church much. But I understood the peace I had in my own soul.

2

The
Primacy of Evangelism

Billy Graham speaks for many churchmen when he says, "It may be the absence of the fear of God and the loss of moral absolutes that sin is accepted and glorified; the breakdown in the home and a disregard for authority; lawlessness; anxiety; hate and bitterness; all give evidence to the signs of cultural decay in our day."

Graham's sentiments about the condition of our nation and our world are echoed daily by hundreds of other clergymen and concerned church leaders.

The world—and the nation—are in flux.

World monetary relationships shift dramatically from the West, where wealth has accumulated for 200 years, to other parts of the globe, especially to the oil-rich Middle East.

Inflation sweeps world-wide; famine stares us in the face. Droughts, floods, calamities drastically threaten the very existence of humankind.

Confronted suddenly by millions of people being overwhelmed by a pervasive mood of pessimism and despair, what does the church do? Nothing—or practically nothing but pontificate. Her message of hope is silent, her answers for life outshouted by voices of perversion and conflict. Her moral responsibilities stilled, her light no longer a beacon, the church hibernates and awaits the spring.

The church must recover its churchhood; the people in Christ, with their common origin and common destiny, must regain their prophetic voice. The gathered church must once again be the place where Christians are empowered, instructed, commissioned and then hurled into the world, able to perform the twofold task of witnessing for Jesus Christ through redemptive presence in the struggles of the world and by verbally calling the world to reconciliation.

The early community of believers evidently was a fellowship that demanded the attention of others because of the qualitative difference of its life. Not only did early Christians speak the message of truth, they also lived it. Their lives illustrated their commitment.

Of how many of us could this be said today?

While Christians are being seduced by their society, the gap between concern and conditioning widens. Committed Christians are becoming a decided minority. The next few years may produce only a handful of believers whose goal is to conquer the whole world with the Good News of Jesus Christ.

And the situation will continue to worsen unless lives changed by the grace of God become living evidence of Jesus, and unless discipleship demands are taken seriously and the gospel is not blunted.

Churches are empty because they offer only a sterile, empty alternative to the world's false front of gaiety and affluence. Non-Christians see too many "mature Christians" as people who know God, know what they believe, but attend church merely for intellectual, aesthetic or social pursuits, or to propagate humanistic philosophy, religious or irreligious, moral or immoral, legal or illegal, theist or atheistic.

Modern man and woman, despite cries for self-sufficiency and self-determination, want to love and be loved; they hunger for something they cannot always explain and understand; they need and want to be comforted by the Supreme Being.

But if Christians exhibit only enough contact with Christ to appease the conscience, the world will never find the love, understanding or comfort Jesus Christ offers.

Therefore, God demands that his churches come to a deep and abiding commitment to their primary task: dynamic evangelism.

Not everything a church does can be called evangelism. Many activities have nothing to do with edifying the saints, much less evangelizing the outsider.

Yet many assume that since the church building has been for so long the center of worship and religious activity, non-Christians will come to it if invited. The New Testament, however, calls for Christians to "go into all the world."

First-century Christians, taking the injunction literally, spread the Christian message through the known world. Twentieth-century Christians must do the same.

If today's church is to grow, it must consist of born-again people who are more committed to "going" than "coming." It must acknowledge evangelism as its top priority; it must mobilize all its resources in a comprehensive witness.

Renewal must take place. Members must get excited about reaching their communities; they must follow a "blind evangelism" that reaches out to every person, self-righteous and sinners, scribes and Pharisees, youth and elderly, Gentile and Jew, socialites and outcasts.

But the issue, says Orlando Costa, is not "how many Christians can be enlisted for action or how the church 'saturates' society with the gospel, rather it is how we get the dynamic organism to grow integrally. How we get this community to be at the same time in the living-worshiping-fellowship, a dynamic training center and an effective team in a complicated world; and how we can put all her structures at the service of the kingdom so that evangelism—the proclamation of the gospel, and the subsequent invitation to confess Jesus Christ as Lord and Savior and be incorporated into the life of his kingdom—will no longer be a superficial, commercial, manipulative whitewash, but a comprehensive enterprise where the gospel is shared in the depth of man's needs and multiple life situations."

The responsibility of the local church is to penetrate its community with Christian leavening. The local church is not about the business of recruiting financial supporters or even internal workers; instead, its need is to view the congregation as an organism, a living body of interacting parts through whom the kingdom reaches out via personal evangelists scattered abroad, bringing people to Jesus Christ.

The effectiveness of a congregation's evangelism depends upon its ability to allow the Holy Spirit to operate unshackled by traditional or idealized structuralism; in such freedom church members can stretch their imaginations and function with a dynamism reminiscent of the early Christians.

God calls his churches to compassionate commitment to personal evangelism; the Scriptures tell us to witness, to take seriously the task of "going into all the world." God wants individuals to proclaim the Good News they've experienced and to follow the New Testament example of continuous, constant dynamic evangelism.

Effective Christians throughout the centuries have followed this pattern of working from the center outward, from the local neighborhood to the far edges of the world. They began next door, moved out from their own to others' home ground. Always driven by the remembrance of Jesus, they took mission as a manner of life.

Michael Green speaks of the early church's evangelism being central to its existence: it was their top priority, based on a compassion for men without Christ. He sees it affecting their relationships with others in numerous ways:

1. The early church people were flexible in their preaching the Good News but utterly opposed to syncretism (mixing other elements with the gospel).

2. They were open to the Holy Spirit's leading in every evangelistic advance.

3. They were not minister-conscious but expected every follower to be a witness for Jesus Christ.

4. They felt church buildings were unimportant; they had none during the period of Christianity's greatest advance; only when church buildings began to take on undue import did religion enter its "dark ages."

5. They felt evangelism was a natural, spontaneous expression of one's commitment to Christ. They practiced apologetics.

6. They went where people were and made disciples of them; they asked no one to "come to us." There was never any thought of meeting someone halfway—they went to them without question, no matter where they were: jails, slums, schools, homes, businesses, synagogues, fields. There was no joy like introducing a friend to Jesus Christ.

7. They frequently discussed the gospel; they were not afraid to talk about their faith in open, philosophical debate—in schools, about town, wherever people were.

8. They seemed to have been able to convert whole communities.

9. They made a maximum impact on society because the maximum impact had been made in
their lives and the quality of their dedication.
The Christian community did not lack commitment.

10. They embraced all colors, all classes, all
people; the untouchables of society mingled
with the elite, sharing a perpetual celebration
in the face of death.

11. They emphasized home fellowships since public meetings were discouraged.

"It is not the church's job," warns evangelist Harold Loucke
in *The Castle in the Field,* "to become a tribe for the improvement and holiness of people who think it would be
pleasant to be holy; a means to the integration of character for
those who cannot bear their conflicts. It is a statement for the
divine intention of humanity."

Today's fellowship has the same responsibility as its Christian ancestors, to be a dynamic organism with a world-wide
imperative of comprehensive witnessing.

If we are to do this, we must reexamine priorities, we must
analyze and evaluate our past and present performances; we
must reflect seriously on God's Word and the best ways to use
the gifts he has given us; for it is time we stopped talking
about evangelism and started acting evangelistically in all our
activities and spheres of life, inside and outside the church. It
is time we get at our task.

The charge of Jesus to his disciples of every generation is
to "go forth therefore and make all nations my disciples,
evangelize the world now."

The challenge is for a dynamic evangelism. Nothing less will
do.

3

Inevitable Evangelism

"The wind blows where it wishes and you hear the sound of it, but do not know where it comes from and where it is going; so is every one who is born of the Spirit." Nicodemus answered and said to Him, "How can these things be?" Jesus answered and said to him, "Are you the teacher of Israel, and do not understand these things? Truly, truly, I say to you, we speak that which we know, and bear witness of that which we have seen; and you do not receive our witness. If I told you earthly things and you do not believe, how shall you believe if I tell you heavenly things?" (John 3:8–12).

3

Prologue

Ada, Oklahoma, was a medium-sized, traditional town when I went to pastor its First Baptist Church.

I didn't want to go. For one thing, it didn't mean a great raise in salary. For another, I was doing fine in Texas. My church was alive; I was active in the community; I loved it.

After my renewal experience, I felt spiritually keener, more sensitive to the needs of my congregation.

But I was also aware, as never before, that God and I were working together. And somehow, I believed, the place he wanted to work was Ada.

I prayed he'd give the church a spiritual awakening.

It happened one Sunday night, some few months after I went there. The Lord walked into that service. We started at 7:00 P.M. We were still going after midnight.

The church was never again the same. While I was there, and during the next pastorate, attendance jumped by two to three hundred; baptisms rose into the hundreds, then hundred-fifties, all seemingly without effort.

The people were witnesses; they practiced the art of Christian sharing. They were evangelistic without being pushed to be.

Before, they'd been acting by the letter of the law; suddenly they began responding to the Spirit of God. It wasn't organization or programs or anything else that gave record numbers of baptisms in Ada; rather it was the people who believed God had the power to change lives.

Once he became the center of their existence, it was easy for them to turn around.

I just helped them be what God had intended them to be. It was the wind of the Spirit.

3

Inevitable Evangelism

Howard Ramsey, an evangelist in the Northwestern states, tells of being confronted by a little woman after a few months in one of his first pastorates.

The woman had a perplexed expression as she told Ramsey, "You've got me in a lot of turmoil, a lot of tension because you keep preaching and teaching that all of us are responsible to go out into the homes and share Christ. Our other pastor told us most of us would make a mess of doing this."

Ramsey laughs about the incident, but not about the problem that underlies it. One of the most difficult assignments facing church leaders today is to get everyone who claims church affiliation to recognize the evangelistic, missionary responsibility they have.

"The company of Jesus is not a people streaming to a shrine, but is laborers engaged in the harvesting task," says Quaker philosopher Elton Trueblood in *The Company of the Committed.* "A person who claims to have a religious experience yet makes no effort to share or expend it has never really entered into Christ's company at all."

Challenged by the overwhelming task of bringing the Good News of Jesus to the world, pastors and laity must walk the same path, each equipped by and equipping the other, each providing a direction and outlet impossible for the other.

Every individual who says "I believe . . ." is part of the family of God with equal authority to bring others into the family.   .

Clearly the minister cannot carry the load alone. Nor did God intend this.

In surveying the work of New Testament Christians, we discover three methods of evangelizing which flowed unconsciously and naturally from the initial conversion experience.

First came personal and collective "good works" conducted in Christ's name which often preceded a verbal explanation of the Christian motivation behind the acts.

A second method of evangelizing was the personal testimony of one believer to another individual.

A third method was public proclamation of the gospel.

People of the New Testament revealed unusual power in both words and deeds, a reflection of the infectious personal relationship they had with Christ. Their enthusiasm in faith was mirrored in their responses to his teachings.

Because they experienced God's love and mercy, they could not help but spread the word that Jesus Christ had died on the cross and been raised again to give assurance to all who would believe the truth.

Church leaders concentrated on public proclamation while individual believers boldly faced their peers with a fierce dedication that became contagious.

In less than three centuries, the early Christians had turned upside down the world they lived in.

At no previous time in history has the church had better prepared, more able leadership. Twentieth-century congregations possess the finest equipment and most comfortable buildings ever known in Christianity's two thousand years.

Yet, amidst the advantages, the church has failed to effectively witness to a lost world.

One reason is that the ministers have not realized, as Howard Ramsey did, the necessity to equip the congregation to do the task.

"The main resources in manpower for evangelism have thus far not been tapped," concludes George Peters. "The great assets of the church are frozen in beautiful cathedrals and buildings. Mobilization of all Christians for evangelism is heard as an occasional slogan, but it is not seen in general practice. The priesthood of all believers has remained a dogma few take seriously. A church of 'we the people' is little believed and experienced."

Even though all Christians should by virtue of their commitment be evangelistic, not every Christian is. Sometimes their failure to witness comes merely because they are unaware of their need to begin; for others it comes because they don't know how to begin.

Confronting others with the Good News of Jesus Christ is not an easy task today. Rejection and hostility are as common a response as welcome and warmth. Christian hesitancy is understandable, but also acceptable. Especially if the church has made an effort to help.

The church that recognizes evangelism as its top priority will not shrink from its responsibility to help its people become conscientious, capable witnesses to their faith. But to accomplish this, preparation is necessary—no, imperative.

No matter how much time and energy it takes to equip the congregation, it is the church's task. The church is God's only appointed instrument for spreading the gospel—there is no other spiritually redeeming agency existing.

For the church, the collective body of Christ, failure to devote itself to the work of evangelism is to condemn itself to a cold and dying ministry outside the fabric of New Testament Christianity.

Evangelism is not the only work the average church should do. But it must be practiced first if the church wants to continue as the living bride of Christ.

Jesus said, "As my Father has sent me, so send I you." And again, "You shall be my witnesses both in Jerusalem, Judea, and to the uttermost part of the earth."

In the *Rebirth of the Ministry,* James D. Smart writes, "The church is in constant danger of unconsciously becoming something other than that which it was founded to be; the body of Christ in which he continues to live and speak and act among men."

The church has only one ultimate aim: to reconcile the world through an understanding of the life and death of the Galilean carpenter. To gain this end, it makes disciples, builds buildings, teaches children, conducts ministries. But if it loses sight of that ultimate aim, it suffers defeat.

Writes Renée Padilla, an international evangelist: "The church is not a religious club that organizes forays into the world in order to gain followers through persuasive technics. It is the sign of the kingdom of God; it lives and proclaims the gospel here and now, among men, and waits for the consummation of God's plan to place all things under the rule of Christ.

"The church has been freed from the world, but it is in the world; it has been sent by Christ into the world just as Christ was sent by the Father.

"In other words, it has been given a mission oriented toward the building of a new humanity in which God's plan for humankind is accomplished, and a mission that can be performed only through sacrifice. Its highest ambition cannot and should not be to achieve the success that leads to triumphalism but rather faithfulness through its Lord which leads it to confess we are unworthy servants; we have only done what was our duty."

George Peters echoes Padilla's concepts. "Ideal New Testament evangelism must build into itself dynamic factors that will bring renewal to the churches, that will add converts to local congregations, that will transmute the event into a movement and that will facilitate the continued gospel ministry to local congregations in the communities."

The Great Commission was not given to professional church staff members but to every Christian, no matter what his or her vocation. The pastor-centered church is challenged by the layperson-centered nature of the mobilization methodology.

Pastors are not only proclaimers and directors with administrative responsibilities, but also leaders with a twofold role: to build an equipping ministry while conducting a proclaiming ministry.

They must teach the concept that the believer's relationship to Christ is a springboard to witnessing. And they should encourage every evangelized person to become an evangelist.

For ultimately, the degree of the gospel's penetration into the world rests not on the pulpit-power of the minister but on the ability of church leaders to inspire church members to total commitment to Christ's demand "to go into all the world."

As the congregation is equipped to witness, the church body is turned on. New life blossoms like spring flowers. What a joy this is to the pastor who finds fulfillment in the pastoral roles of shepherd, the feeder of the people, and teacher, equipper of the congregation.

Unfortunately, the task of equipping isn't as easy as many believe it. The pastor of a large Southern Baptist church tells of his gradual acceptance of this responsibility and his congregation's response.

One, speaking the sentiment of many, told the pastor, "We

pay you to be the minister, and I expect you to do what we hire you for. If you were sick, you wouldn't want me to send an assistant, a novice, to attend you. You pay for my services, and I respond.

"Well," the individual concluded, slightly angry, "we pay for your services the same way."

That attitude may be heard in congregations that have by-passed the New Testament example of the church to lock-in on the twentieth-century program of activities and projects.

The object of today's church is not to maintain the Wednesday night supper or get a large crowd to attend the boys' basketball game. The object of today's church is to reach the individual who needs Christ's message of hope. And anything that stands between the church and that object—goals, plans, calendar dates, expenditures or resources—should be reexamined.

The struggle to motivate a congregation satiated by the frivolous "norms of the church today" can be taxing, but it is necessary. For motivated people witness. They extend the church's outreach far beyond the abilities of the paid staff.

Excited by their intimate relationship to Jesus, a committed congregation shares him freely and seeks better ways of telling his story.

But people without motivation, no matter how much they know or how many "successful" approaches they learn, will not effectively witness over the long run.

Fred White, director of evangelism for Maryland Southern Baptists, has said, "The pastor is to develop full-grown, mature Christians who will be motivated by the spirit of God to become consistent, effective witnesses for Jesus Christ. Motivation to witness stems from our relationship to Christ. Apart from our vital connection with him through faith, there can be no valid motivation.

"Every child of God should have an inner compulsion to

witness as the Apostle Paul expressed in 1 Corinthians 9:16*b:*
'For I am compelled to preach the Gospel by order of my
Master, for woe is me if I do not preach the Gospel.' "

Motivation is critical. The brevity of life and the judgment
of God upon sinners, the horrors of hell and the glory of
heaven, the promise of his coming all create urgency for the
Christian witness.

Equipping people is an unending task. No congregation is
ever fully equipped but always in the process of being equipped
—until every member of the church feels witnessing the essence
of his life and the theme around which his life-style is written.

Compassion for others, an awareness of the lateness of the
hour, a sense of Christian perspective all play a part in moti-
vating the believer to witness.

And once motivated, evangelistic endeavors flow naturally
from him or her. But dynamic, successful evangelism has something else going for it: thorough, skillful, God-led training.

Its effectiveness is grounded in knowledge, matured in the
Word of God, encouraged by the fellowship of like-minded
Christians. It rests easy on the individual believer's ability to
daily recognize or create opportunities for sharing verbally
with those who do not know Christ.

Obviously such training does not discount the need for the
leadership and presence of the Holy Spirit. Such training does
make the Christian a more effective instrument for disseminat-
ing God's message in the world.

New Testament evangelism is achievable. If in the circumstances of the first century, people could do it, so can succeed-
ing generations.

Evangelism can be as much a way of life in the 1970s as it
was in the A.D. 70s. "It is not like the commands of the day,
a command which men are impenitent to obey," says Harry
R. Boer in *Pentecost and Missions.* "It is a command which
has been given because the church has the power to obey it,

because the spirit has been given to the church, because it is of her essence and nature to be a witnessing body."

The task of evangelizing the world passes from generation to generation; it becomes our moral and spiritual obligation, our unassailable responsibility.

When J. B. Phillips translated the Book of Acts, he described those early Christians' actions in words that should apply to church people today. "The new-born church as vulnerable as any human child having neither money, influence, nor power in the ordinary sense, is setting forth joyfully and courageously to win the pagan world for God through Christ. It is vigorous and flexible, for those are the days before it ever became fat and short of breath through prosperity or muscle bound by over-organization. These men did not make acts of faith. They believed. They did not say their prayers; they really prayed. They did not hold conferences on psychosomatic medicine. They simply healed the sick. . . .

"There is something here at work besides mere human beings. It is a matter of sober, historical fact that never before has any small body of ordinary people so moved the world that their enemies could say with tears of rage in their eyes that these men had turned the world upside down."

So let the equipped church move out under the challenge of reaching a world for Christ. May the wind of the Spirit breathe upon us. And caught by that mighty breath, may we experience *inevitable evangelism.*

4

Evangelism—
the Spark and the Fire

And that you be renewed in the spirit of your mind, and put on
the new self, which in the likeness of God has been created
in righteousness and holiness of the truth. Therefore, laying aside
falsehood, speak truth, each one of you, with his neighbor, for we
are members of one another. Be angry, and yet do not sin;
do not let the sun go down on your anger, and do not give the
devil an opportunity. Let him who steals steal no longer; but rather
let him labor, performing with his own hands what is good, in
order that he may have something to share with him who has need.
Let no unwholesome word proceed from your mouth, but
only such a word as is good for edification according to the need of
the moment, that it may give grace to those who hear. And do not
grieve the Holy Spirit of God, by whom you were sealed for
the day of redemption. Let all bitterness and wrath and anger
and clamor and slander be put away from you, along with
all malice (Eph. 4:23–31).

4

Prologue

I have always had a hunger for knowledge. But it wasn't until seminary that I really learned the pleasure of study. I had made "A" and "B" grades in high school and college. But in seminary, I began working for knowledge's sake, not for grades.

I read everything I could. I never lost my belief in the Bible, its inspiration or its truths. But I swung toward a liberal stance. Barth, Bultmann, Tillich began to affect my preaching and my concepts.

I shunned revivals; I preached from the head, not the heart.

Then I was called to pastor a little church out in the Texas Panhandle. It was one of the best things that ever happened to me.

Happy, Texas, had about 700 residents: storekeepers, bankers, farmers, and ranchers. Many were college-educated. They demanded a preacher who'd produce.

I became an activist, joining clubs and civic organizations, working for community development and economic improvement. I was a pusher, and I pushed the church. It grew; just about doubled in attendance.

If a pastor is going to reach people, he ought not to live in a cloistered tower. He needs to be where the people are. I was there, involved in everything, from fighting liquor to working to improve treatment of juveniles who had been arrested.

From Happy I moved to First Baptist Church, Post, Texas. I was there six years, in something of a repeat performance of my life at Happy. Again, I was active in the community; again the church grew.

My concern for social issues was strong. I worked to bring blacks into the associational fellowship. I have a daughter who is Korean, so I have deep feelings about justice and equality of all people.

Yet what I was doing was more a physical effort than a spiritual effort. I was a tireless worker, one of those men driven to succeed.

I was building a reputation. But I was doing it all on my own steam.

Then I accepted the pastorate of Crescent Park Baptist Church in Odessa. I spent several years there. And there I had renewal—personal renewal.

I came to Odessa intent on following old patterns. But what had worked in Happy and Post now sent me into eighteen-hour work days and the feeling that everything was coming down around me.

When a minor recession hit the oil industry—and our community was heavily peopled by oil company workers —we began losing people in droves. The church had to have sixteen visitors each week to stay even. The situation was down-hill sledding.

Because I'd always been successful, I thought I was responsible. I worked harder and harder. But I felt dry. I had enough personality to get people to keep joining the church. But I was finding the work more and more frustrating.

Many days, I was to the point of quitting.

I explored other jobs, both in and out of the ministry. I felt such an emptiness.

Some of the church staff were aware of my tensions,

few members were. I didn't share this or my feelings with them.

About this time we had a retreat that featured C. L. Culpepper, the missionary to China, who'd been through the great spiritual awakening that his country experienced before World War II.

Culpepper laid it on. He talked about sin in our lives, about problems in relationship to others.

I had gone to the retreat only because I was in charge; I hadn't wanted to go. Culpepper made me sorry I had. He hurt my feelings. He made me mad.

I hadn't committed murder, hadn't stolen or committed adultery. I had an unblemished record on the "big sins." But I couldn't get away from the feeling that some other real sins were overwhelming my life.

I didn't pray much in those days, didn't read the Bible often, except to get a sermon passage or clarify a point. But I wanted to pray. I decided to closet myself in my little study.

To get my attention, God really had to clobber me.

I said, "I've got to get in or get out, God, totally, all the way." I poured myself out to him. I asked him to reveal my problems and my needs.

He did. I was a hypocrite. I made out I was something I wasn't. I had some bad relationships with people; some bills I hadn't paid.

I asked forgiveness. And I began to try to right the relationships I knew to be wrong. But I still wasn't satisfied.

Later, I went back to the study, shut the door, turned out the light. I fell on my face and said, "God, I am going to wrestle with you until I have finished this thing. I'm staying here until it's done."

I don't know how long I was there.

But I felt, somehow, as if the room was just totally in the light of God. God got me by the nape of the neck, turned me up by the heels and just emptied me, like a woman turning her purse upside down and dumping out the contents. Then I felt he just poured himself into me.

I didn't jump up and speak in tongues. I didn't race out to find someone to lay hands on and heal. But that was the day I really surrendered to God in the fullness of ministry. I knew him. I had matured. I didn't run around with it on my lapel, but I was different; my friends, my family, my church all knew it.

I was me. *No longer liberal or conservative. Merely a follower of Christ. I don't ever want to go back to the way I was the day before I had that renewal experience. I quit struggling and found peace in sweet surrender.*

4

Evangelism— the Spark and the Fire

Perhaps no word has been used more often—or more loosely—by evangelists and religious leaders than the word *revival*. Originally, revival called people to a new life experience, a time of renewing the human spirit amidst a world of restlessness and general dissatisfaction, of despair and ungodly conditions. Revival challenged Christians to once again inculcate their society with the values of Christian conversion, the joys of Christian service and the excitement of the Christian journey.

Through the years, however, revival has come to have a more limited definition. Its most common usage today is as an evangelistic campaign. And for many, it has also come to connote a somewhat suspicious, Elmer Gantry-style "fly-by-night tent religion."

The unfortunate modern connotations of revival have led evangelism strategists to acknowledge the validity of the original "revival experience" but to call it "renewal," to focus people's attention on the moment, not the meeting.

Renewal evangelism therefore concentrates on the individual's need to revitalize—or renew—his or her Christian commitment.

Descriptions of the renewal experience have included "the holy fire falling," "the breathing of the divine breath," "the outpouring of the Holy Spirit," "God with us," "great manifestations of God's presence," "the effusion of the Holy Spirit," "the refreshing influence of divine grace," and scores of others. Each attempts to explain a feeling that is essentially inexplicable; the regaining of new life for a Christian.

Today a new emphasis on personal commitment and an evidence of religious awakening are taking place. Christian philosopher Elton Trueblood has described the burgeoning movement as the "most hopeful Christian development of our generation, a viable alternative to both apathy and despair."

The renewal experience is vital to the church's life, a part of its total outreach and of its thrilling thrust into the world. Shallow, superficial, external religion offers little to attract anyone. Today's faith must center on the meaning of life and the dynamic essence of an experimental relationship to God.

If God means anything, twentieth-century human beings demand to see that meaning in the life of believers.

By virtue of his living, breathing walk through this world, every Christian is a witness. But the question plaguing Christianity today is, "To what is he a witness?"—his joyful experience with God? Or his lack of concern about God's message to humankind?

If members of the fellowship of believers hide in the comfort of structured buildings, the answer is clear.

To demonstrate the power of God, the people of God must get out of their "religion stands" on the corner and, wherever they are, respond to the world with the enthusiastic joy that derives from a living relationship with Jesus Christ.

"The trouble with most unhappy and unfruitful Christians is that they are living a subnormal life," writes R. Q. Leavell in *Evangelism: Christ's Imperative Commission*. "A revival is not an abnormal time, but rather it is a time when Christians are brought up to the normal activities, the normal victory and the normal happiness which should prevail perennially."

Renewal evangelism may be the spark to kindle this "normal" fire in the hearts and lives of God's people.

Already a powerful pulsation of renewal based on New Testament patterns and under constructive, guiding control of the Holy Spirit is sweeping the United States like a swelling wave. Hopefully it will rise to a crest which washes over the entire breadth of church life.

If it does, life-style evangelism will spontaneously erupt that points out the importance of attitudinal, relational, incarnational Christianity, an evangelism which speaks of living out the Christ "in you" in daily circumstances. It will be an evangelism in which one sheds personal hangups to be free, to be open with other believers in the greatest fellowship experience available to human beings.

But such an experience with renewal evangelism seldom occurs without individual preparation. Indeed, a restudy of Christian conversion is needed for it is almost impossible to move into this deeper relationship without honestly coming to grips with the God-directed purpose of life.

Evangelism of renewal calls for godly living. Flippantly to dissipate one's relationship to God for human desires will not make a life which conveys the beauty of God or gives evidence of God's joyous meaning of life; nor will such an existence speak clearly of the work of God.

Jesus said, "If I be lifted up, I will draw all men to me." Renewal evangelism emphasizes what Jesus taught about the effectiveness of a life centered on him; it reenforces the importance of the Christ-life on interpersonal relationships.

Living righteously means living for others as well as for God. As a result of renewal, church members affirm God, affirm their brothers and sisters in Christ, affirm their church and denomination, and affirm those who are not Christians.

For Christian renewal, says George Peters, "fellowship must constitute the quality and evangelism must be the purpose, while friendship and neighborliness born out of spiritual concern for the welfare of others must create an atmosphere of total selling."

Renewal evangelism deepens an individual's concern for others in the dynamics of a renewed fellowship—believers explode with an infectious spirit of energetic witnessing.

"God's Spirit has been moving in a mighty and wonderful way in our church as a result of our lay renewal weekend," says Jack Clifford, pastor of a Hyattsville, Maryland, church.

"On the closing Sunday night, more than one hundred people came to share, pray, testify, and sing for almost three hours. Men and women and youth were laughing, crying, embracing, praising God! Normally shy men and women were leaping to their feet and expressing needs and victories.

"Youth and adults joined together and the generation gap was closed," Clifford continues. "People were reconciling themselves to one another and middle walls of partition crumbled. It was truly a day that will stand at the height of my Christian experience."

Clearly the journey outward toward a life-style of evangelism begins with the journey inward toward a renewal of self.

Renewed Christians do not adjust their timetables to a frenzied and hurried society; they move in the midst of their culture to tell the Good News.

The experience of renewal usually manifests itself in an individual's increased efforts to:

1. lead lost people to find personal salvation through faith in Christ;
2. lead Christian people to find a deeper relation-

ship with Christ and a deeper commitment to
him; and
3. work to enable the fellowship of believers to find
ways of leading other laypersons to a deeper expression of their Christian faith.

Because evangelism leaders became aware of the exciting
new life-styles that result from the renewal experience, they began studying renewal evangelism.

Although aware that the experience can be "programed" out
of existence, evangelism strategists discovered that most people
who find renewal go through five phases that move from initial
investigation to penetration in the community.

They then began to hammer out a program that would include these phases, giving churches a well-diagramed approach
to the renewal experience. The program they developed includes:

Phase one—investigation: At a church's invitation, a trained
renewal evangelism consultant visits the pastor and church
leaders to discuss renewal needs. Following this "listening
visit," the consultant suggests methods of involving the church
in renewal.

Phase two—initiation: After investigation, church leaders
plan the first renewal event, often a "lay renewal weekend."
Lay persons from other churches visit the host church for a
weekend of sharing their faith.

Phase three—exploration: Small search groups are formed.
The groups offer opportunities to explore for each individual
his or her awareness of the Holy Spirit and for each to build
stronger relationships with fellow Christians.

Phase four—celebration: As the renewal experience takes
hold, lay people need a time to express their differing inter-
pretations of the new life and its spiritual implications on the

fellowship. On a renewal celebration weekend a team of visitors from other churches, local church members, a team coordinator and a learning session leader channel the church through the tensions and potentials that surface into positive directions for its new life under the Lordship of Jesus.

Phase five—penetration: In a six-month study of the public ministry of Jesus, participants identify with Jesus' ministry and consider its implications for their own lives.

In the experience of renewal evangelism strategists, the overt results of this intensive small group study have been a heightened desire by participants to penetrate the world in mission action and to increase their skill in personal witnessing.

After a renewal weekend at Broadacres Baptist Church in Shreveport, Louisiana, for example, Pastor Don Fletcher reports a four-and-a-half-hour Sunday evening service during which:

- 35 people volunteered to be used as team members for lay renewal weekends;
- 30 homes were opened for prayer, Bible study and sharing groups;
- 13 volunteered for the bus ministry;
- 8 volunteered to work in a KOA campground ministry;
- 61 asked to be part of a sharing group;
- 20 committed themselves to leading groups at the church;
- 32 expressed an interest in training for more intensive evangelistic outreach.

"Our church will never be the same again," says Fletcher. "I don't know what tomorrow holds for us, but this I know: every pastor, deacon and church leader in every church should schedule a lay renewal weekend in their church. Oh, how we need to get out of our lives and our churches the dryness, the deadness, the old deadly routine that kills Holy Spirit power."

Dozens of others have expressed similar emotions.

For Bill and Betty Myers of Stone Mountain, Georgia, the weekend helped them discover that "God wanted more from us than our work in his church. He wanted us to be alive, free Christians committed to him. A loving Lord who knew how tired our spirits were spoke to us that weekend and refreshed our souls.

"That weekend was the beginning of many changes in our lives," the Myerses say.

Perhaps that "new day for Christ" has been the most important result of the lay renewal experience for within such growing awareness has come a surging current of caring for others and hearing this newly understood love for one another. It is an experience of persons who, often for the first time, are giving themselves openly and with vulnerability to others.

"I had come to a point where I didn't care if all my fellow workers knew I was a Christian," admits Joe Chalk, a layperson in the First Baptist Church of Tucker, Georgia.

"At church, I would say I am proud to be a Christian, but at the office, I just wouldn't tell anyone."

After attending a lay renewal weekend, Chalk overcame his hurdle of shyness and found he "loved the Lord more than I cared what people thought about me." He started a prayer breakfast at work. In less than a year, more than one hundred and fifty people had attended the once-weekly meeting, with an average attendance of thirty-five.

"God has used me and the chance for Christians to identify with each other to strengthen the lives of all who attend," Chalk says.

As exemplified by Chalk, the Myerses and thousands of others, the full renewal experience demonstrates total, honest commitment in the lives of everyday people who know Jesus as Lord—businessmen, teachers, housewives, doctors, students, scientists, insurance salesmen, mechanics who are living the Good News of Christ in the life-giving, redemptive fellowship of believers. Renewal is the journey from struggle to surrender.

5

God's Liberation Movement

So Moses went out and told the people the words of the Lord. Also, he gathered seventy men of the elders of the people, and stationed them around the tent. Then the Lord came down in the cloud and spoke to him; and He took of the Spirit who was upon him and placed Him upon the seventy elders. And it came about that when the Spirit rested upon them, they prophesied. But they did not do it again. But two men had remained in the camp, the name of one was Eldad and the name of the other Medad. And the Spirit rested upon them (now they were among those who had been registered, but had not gone out to the tent), and they prophesied in the camp. So a young man ran and told Moses and said "Eldad and Medad are prophesying in the camp." Then Joshua the son of Nun, the attendant of Moses from his youth, answered and said, "Moses, my lord, restrain them." But Moses said to him, "Are you jealous for my sake? Would that all that Lord's people were prophets, that the Lord would put His Spirit upon them!" (Num. 11:24–29).

5

Prologue

I had been pastoring in Ada, Oklahoma, for less than a year and a half when the Oklahoma Baptist Convention asked me to become director of evangelism for the state.

I didn't want the job. I thought you only went into state or denominational work if you couldn't do anything else.

Again God clobbered me. I took the job.

I was already enthusiastic about some of the things being done in evangelism, especially the renewed emphasis on lay witness.

Lay evangelism fits into my own thinking about the way lay people should be involved. There is a great deal of joy in sharing one's faith if it's possible to do so freely without feeling that every time one goes out he has to get another notch on his spiritual gun.

It's not important to be able to shoot the eyes out of an argument with your spiritual acumen; what's important is when the smoke clears away, how many folks are at the feet of Jesus.

We started concentrating on lay evangelism schools.

People who attended them were excited because afterwards they could witness in the office, in school, in the homes of friends, with a freedom they'd never felt before.

I remember one little lady attending the school for the first time who said to me, "I'm not going visiting on Thursday night; I'm chicken."

She was nervous about it all week. But on Thursday she mustered her courage and went out. She was instrumental in leading someone to Christ that night; she came back so elated and exuberant. She was never "chicken" again.

On another occasion some young people had gone out and led about twenty people to Christ. A senior in high school, tall and skinny, vivacious with excitement, came back saying, "I just don't believe I can wait until tomorrow to witness, I'm going back out again tonight."

He walked out and did just that.

Sometimes people have hangups about using the printed materials we recommend. In an Oklahoma City lay school a college boy told me, "I can't use that booklet, I'll just tell the people what Jesus did for me."

On his first visit, he faced another youngster about his own age. The first thing he did was to give his testimony. Then he stammered. He didn't know what to do next.

"I got flustered," he told me later, "so I just pulled out the little book."

The two young men went through the booklet which details the plan of salvation, and the one being visited listened. After prayer, he said, "Yes, I accept Jesus."

That young man came back so beside himself, the first thing he said was, "I want a hundred more of those little books." A little book which was a simple little tool was used of God to set a lay person free. This is what it's all about. For him a hard job was transformed into a heart throb—a tool and a challenge.

5

God's Liberation Movement

Hidden behind brick walls and stained-glass windows in the security of their mediocrity, many churches have not been excited about God's command: "You shall be my witnesses both in Jerusalem, Judea and in Samaria, and in the uttermost parts of the earth."

Personal evangelism has no "come-and-hear" strategy. Admittedly, we must not surrender public proclamation of the Word. Yet we must be so intensely identified with Christ; so involved with him, that we eagerly "go-and-tell."

Reaching people is the foremost priority of every member of every church. Evangelism is the unrelenting responsibility of every follower of Jesus. But not every believer witnesses verbally of Jesus' power to change lives.

In *Our Guilty Silence,* John R. W. Stott says, "The causes of our guilty silence are (1) either we have no compelling incentive even to try to speak, or (2) we do not know what to say, or (3) we are not convinced that it is our job, or (4) we do not believe we shall do any good because we have forgotten the source of power."

When Jesus gave his Great Commission, it was not limited to pastors or the "professional ministry." Jesus' last words were to all his disciples. Christians who find themselves with non-Christians—the majority of people met in daily life—are to witness of Christ.

That is Christ's simple command.

There is no substitute for a friend telling a friend what Jesus can do; the lay person speaks the language of his or her craft or profession; he or she understands the circumstances of the world in which people live.

The Christian is not of this world, but he is in it; he can make the world real to those around him. He is not commissioned merely to build church buildings, however necessary they may be in fulfilling community ministry, but he is commissioned to win the lost to Christ and to establish the new believer in the faith.

When church members witness, they experience a new excitement; all of the powers of Satan and darkness cannot stop the advance.

A committed minority within a church can make a powerful impact on the community. But motivation is not enough; motivation does wonders, but it does not take the place of skills.

For years, lay people have needed more specific and practical assistance in becoming effective witnesses. Handicapped too long by inferiority, minority, defeatist complexes, lay people have hesitated to go exploit witnessing opportunities. Because of a lack of training and experience, they have held back when the proper course would have been bold attack.

Recognizing the situation, evangelism planners devised a program to equip lay people for witnessing. As a remedy for doubtful discipleship, it has been amazingly successful.

This program is the lay evangelism school. Lay evangelism schools have helped turn hundreds of thousands of timid or ineffective witnesses into skillful, sure practitioners of "lifestyle evangelism." Using small group experiences as an approach to training, the schools give trainees the actual experience of witnessing but under the direction and supervision of experts.

The schools are not designed to replace commitment, nor do they downplay the need for the presence of the Holy Spirit in all witnessing activities. To perceive them as the means by which a person comes to know Christ is to come perilously close to loosing New Testament evangelism in twentieth-century techniques.

The schools are simply opportunities for lay people who are motivated to witness to sharpen their witnessing abilities.

The spiritual objectives of lay evangelism schools are:

1. to help Christians experience a full and meaningful life in Jesus Christ;
2. to have Christians share their testimony for Jesus in simple and effective ways;
3. to help Christians know how to train others in sharing their testimony for Christ;
4. to help the church see the nature of its priority task in training and equipping Christians for a life of witness and involvement for Jesus Christ; and
5. to help the church establish continuing witness training and involvement for its members.

The lay evangelism school is not just the same old program with a new name. It emphasizes being and doing. Trained teachers who have themselves had the spiritual experience of the school offer content that strikes a balance between spiritual motivation and practical activities. Teaching methods include lectures, groups dynamics, practical lab and field experiences in witnessing.

These are all evaluated for the group and each individual.

The quick and ready acceptance of the lay evangelism schools by churches and church groups has proved their importance in filling a witnessing vacuum.

From the first, mission strategists undertook the project with three basic convictions.

The first conviction was that the greatest need in training lay people is building adequate spiritual foundations. No set of materials no matter how "slick" would make evangelists out of the laity. No strategy no matter how carefully devised would evangelize this generation.

This bedrock of all witnessing experiences must be spiritual power which comes only when people rediscover the wellsprings of faith and hope that Jesus offers. To call persons to once again turn to the source of their existence was the first goal of the schools' planners.

The second conviction was that the greatest asset in training lay people for evangelism is the local church. From the beginning, lay school strategists determined that training for lay evangelism, including leadership training, should be done in the context of a local congregation.

The third conviction was the need for basic materials to aid the process of lay training and to aid the actual witnessing experience. A series of Bible-centered tracts and pamphlets was produced. They are simple, adaptable and thorough.

Mission strategists also had some basic convictions about the schools they were proposing. Among the qualities they wanted were schools that were church-centered, conducted in the community where participants lived; and schools that focused on two things: a Bible and a pupil.

Planners wanted also to make the schools growth-oriented and experimental. Pupils needed to learn to communicate their personal experiences, and they needed an opportunity to practice what they had been learning.

Evangelism strategists decided to "test market" their proposed schools in a series of meetings across the United States.

In the first phase, lay school planners conducted experimental lay evangelism schools in only a few areas. These found resounding acceptance which led to a series of others. The lay schools quickly multiplied as more and more individuals were trained to conduct them; churches all across the United States, from Alaska to Florida, began holding lay evangelism schools. In only a few years, literally hundreds of thousands of people had attended lay evangelism schools.

These schools now held in almost all of the fifty states have proved again and again that once Christians discover the joy and freedom of living a life that is full and meaningful, once they know how to communicate their experience to others in simple and effective ways, they will witness. And they will train others to witness.

Today the lay evangelism schools are being held in more churches than ever before. Each includes preparation, training and continuation—the basic ingredients of a successful school.

Once a church decides to hold a lay evangelism school, certain activities are recommended.

Before the school begins, its teachers and the local church leaders spend the time building spiritual foundations, preregistering church members for lay witness training, and locating and cultivating persons who will receive a witness visit during the school's laboratory stages.

The preparation period is presented in two ways. A simplified version covers a twelve-week time-span and involves only the pastor, general director and/or one or more teachers. Some basic assignments may be made to others, but they are less detailed and require less time and money expended.

The second plan takes eighteen weeks. Instructions outline

a week-by-week countdown which requires the pastor and seven directors, all of whom have definite duties.

Vital to the school's success is the development of a "prospects list" at this time. Trainees will visit these unchurched people during the school. Locating prospects can be done through telephone survey or other canvassing methods. But they must be located; without a current propects list the school's effectiveness will be crippled.

Prospects should be classified: nonbelievers, believers without a church home, etc.

Lay evangelism schools normally run 7:00-9:00 P.M. for five days except Thursday, the "witnessing night." Each of the evening sessions has three periods after the introductory time. First period is Bible study with topics, such as "The New Life," "The Cleansed and Controlled Life," "The Witnessing Life," and "The Growing Life." The second period provides creative activities in which participants face honestly their own spiritual inadequacies and discover through group dynamics what to do about them. Third period presents practical activities that help participants learn to share their personal testimony, visit a home, use their Bible and the booklet "A Full and Meaningful Life" in witnessing.

On Thursday evening trainees are divided into groups which engage in actual witnessing experiences with the non-Christians who have been previously classified on the prospects list. After the visits trainees return to share their experiences with the others. Churches often find this one of the week's most exciting and thrilling moments. Coming together in the circle of joyful fellowship undergirds trainees and encourages them to continue witnessing efforts.

Although formal classes end on Friday, the lay school should not conclude then. For it would be of little value if follow-through did not take place. If we properly prepare for a lay evangelism school, conduct it correctly, then allow its activities to die, we've probably produced, in Shakespeare's words, something "full of sound and fury, signifying nothing."

And the school will die, if we play "wait and see."

After observing hundreds of schools, lay witness strategists have discovered the continual witnessing activities are necessary to sustain the momentum built by the school. Therefore, other training experiences, led by persons with witness leadership training, should follow the school.

As with the schools, these activities should concentrate on the one-to-one relationship building necessary to reach individuals for Christ.

The command to win those without Jesus to him and establish them in the faith was given more than two thousand years ago; yet around us are millions of people who have never heard the Good News.

Alone, no one of us can reach the world; but each of us can witness to people we encounter daily. This is one-to-one evangelism that concentrates on persons, not unseen masses of people.

In work, school, leisure, each of us daily talks to persons who need Christ; but do we ever talk to them about Christ? We possess a life-giving message. And the unique contribution of the lay evangelism school is they equip the laity to penetrate the world to a degree far greater than could be done if witnessing were the sole province of the professional church worker.

6

Evangelism, Youth, and Change

Thus incurring condemnation, because they have set aside their previous pledge. And at the same time they also learn to be idle, as they go around from house to house; and not merely idle, but also gossips and busybodies, talking about things not proper to mention. Therefore, I want younger widows to get married, bear children, keep house, and give the enemy no occasion for reproach; for some have already turned aside to follow Satan. If any woman who is a believer has dependent widows, let her assist them, and let not the church be burdened, so that it may assist those who are widows indeed (1 Tim. 5:12–16).

Prologue

I have three sons in college and one in medical school. Maybe because of them, I've always felt that I had a good rapport with young people.

In Oklahoma, we had a television program that used college kids in many of the production numbers—music, skits, etc. Then, at the end of the program, I eyeballed the audience for four or five minutes.

We had fantastic response.

In one audience survey on three college campuses we found three of every four television sets were tuned to our program.

At first the station put us on a trial basis. We preempted the first thirty minutes of Dick Cavett. After the response began coming in, we were scheduled permanently.

Working with the kids was great. You can always be yourself with kids.

In one church we began reaching high school youth. I had sixty-five students committed for special service. I had sixteen who dedicated their lives to the ministry at one time in one church.

I guess we were the "in" church.

But the kids themselves helped make it happen.

If all the young people in the Southern Baptist Convention—or any other denomination—were turned on for Jesus, it would radically alter the life-style of the nation.

And it can happen. Youth are natural; they talk about the things that mean the most to them.

When they know Jesus, they talk about him. They share him. It's that simple. It happened in the first months of the decade of the seventies. It just happened. Serendipity!

6

Evangelism,
Youth, and Change

The 1960s was a crisis decade in America. Technological advances occurred so rapidly that social advances could not keep abreast. Economic uncertainty, social unrest, emotional instability and a spiritual decadence all brought discontent, confusion, tension.

Internal strife rocked the period.

Probably no group was more embroiled in the turmoil than the nation's youth, a generation born of war and never weaned of nuclear pressures.

One expert noted, "Controversial political candidates, social reformers, a U.S. senator and one U.S. president were shot to death by crazed assassins. Colleges, churches, and private homes were burned to the ground and inhabitants summarily executed by vigilantes who had long before substituted violence and lawlessness for reason and due process. . . .

"Radical departures from heretofore unquestioned norms came about," he continued. "Terms like 'H,' 'sugar,' 'acid,' 'grass,' 'junk,' 'high,' and 'trip' shot across the front pages of newspapers, appeared in best-selling books and flashed onto motion picture and television screens with meanings quite different from those found in the dictionary.

77

"The age of Aquarius was suddenly here, heralded by Timothy Leary and 'Hair'—and, almost at once, permissive living, free love and homosexuality were all right. Situation ethics was a term that allowed us to have our cake and eat it too. Satan worship and astrology zoomed into popularity practically overnight, and to American youth of the '60s, suddenly it appeared God was dead."

More than 30 million people between the ages of fifteen and twenty-three years live in America; this is the greatest number of youth in U.S. history. With more than one-seventh of the nation's population below twenty-five and more than half the world's population under twenty-one, our churches must give attention to the problems and needs of youth.

Despite the Jesus Movement and related trends that developed in the early 1970s, more youth than ever before do not know Jesus Christ. But they are reachable.

In fact, statistics reveal that youth are the most susceptible age group. After a person finishes high school and college, the possibility of reaching him or her with the Christian message is cut in half. At young adulthood, it halves again; in middle age, it again halves.

Certainly waiting decreases the chances of success in propagating Christian thought among the nation's people. But reaching youth requires special approaches, special techniques, for today's youth are better educated and healthier than any other generation. Because they will live longer, they want to know what life will bring—and they expect it immediately.

Youth is a time of experimentation; young people want to test their senses. But major problems can result. Among them are drugs, sex, and alcoholism.

A recent survey showed an astounding upsurge in youth alcoholism. A counselor in an alcoholics mission in Pensacola, Florida, recently said that the largest percentage of addicts he counseled were youth between ages fifteen and twenty-three.

Problems stemming from alcoholism, he said, include relationships to parents, lack of sensitivity to needs of the individual in his work, a search for identity and challenge for life.

Drugs continue to ravage youth.

Marijuana, in particular, has been condoned by parents, community leaders, and even religious leaders. Yet recent scientific data indicates marijuana may cause brain damage and/or hormonal imbalance. Further research is necessary before it will be proved as dangerous as cigarette smoking which has been labeled a health hazard because of the high incidence of cancer among smokers.

The drug scene begins in the junior high school years, and passes from "pot" to "hard stuff" all too quickly. Unless youth are offered an alternative to pot parties and quick highs, many will end up with lives ruined by addiction to drugs that destroy the mind and body.

As with alcoholism and drugs, free love and homosexuality are emerging patterns of conduct for youth. Said a recent university graduate, "I don't care what anyone says, the bedrock issue is sex. Students are gripped with man as a natural being, a biological creature with biological needs which are aggravated by social stimuli. The present existential satisfaction of these is all that matters. What is good, what's nice, is good for you. The basic issue thus becomes personal freedom along with the nature and the responsibility of man."

With such prevalent attitudes, youth have little hope unless someone helps them discover meaning on the other side of dehumanization and manipulation.

Unfortunately for most of us, the someone offering help can't be a hypocritical adult who does one thing and proclaims another moral value. Youth are sensitive to the genuine and turned off by the superficial. No wonder American young people appear, in general, alienated and uncommitted. For most youth, life is disordered and out of sync. Existence seems an absurdity in a universe with a closed system which is empty, impersonal and godless.

Youth are searching. Their gropings among the drugs-sex-alcoholism cultures reveal a misdirected quest for purpose and meaning and order. They want fulfillment, but most are lost in an overwhelming sea of circumstances.

"It is of utmost importance that we help them find the faith to live by, achieve a self fit to live with, discover a cause to live for, and cooperate with them in building a world fit to live in," says Jesse Bader in *Evangelism in a Changing America*.

Churches can circumvent many problems, but the churches must be willing to change. Vibrant programs of Bible study and significant opportunities for self-giving service must replace the deplorable exclusiveness of insensitive congregations.

Today's churches must open wide their doors with new warmth and understanding, with new openness and freedom for the expression of Christian love and joy.

A goal of every church should be to help youth find full opportunity for self-expression while developing a maturing life-style relationship to Christ.

Adult leadership is absolutely important. Adults who take responsibility in working with youth are the models of love that young people need to see. Loren Cunningham, a church leader in South Africa, told a group of youth sponsors recently, "The Lord has a unique vision and experience for you as a leader. As you pass your test, God's authority will come to you; but don't stop there, go on and allow God to multiply your experience through others.

"Leaders simply go first and then lead others through the same phase of growth. Never ask them to do what you yourself have never accomplished. This was and is Christ's method to get laborers to disciple them and to send them into the harvest fields of the world.

"As this is accomplished in the family atmosphere of fellowship and love, all the spiritual, social, psychological and personal needs of each worker can be met in the process of world evangelism."

The following four steps prepare the adult to effectively lead youth to their own Christ-experience.

1. Discover and experience the real life of Jesus and a fresh awareness of the Holy Spirit.
2. Build a deeper daily fellowship with Jesus Christ and a more meaningful fellowship in the church, its life, worship, ministry and programs.
3. Share testimony for Jesus in a simple and effective way everywhere.
4. Know how to train others in a witnessing lifestyle.

Adults fit into a youth evangelism strategy in two specific ways. They lead youth to conduct an in-depth ministry to other young people, and they help youth plan a witnessing strategy for every location where youth find themselves today.

Youth evangelism has four suggested areas of study: preparation, leadership group (sometimes called leadership family) training, the week or weekend of training, and growth and outreach.

Preparation builds the foundation upon involvement and practical application. Four Bible passages are studied during this four-week period.

Leadership group training builds a corps of adult leaders who care about and are willing to involve themselves in the lives of young people on a continuing basis. The training lasts twelve weeks.

The youth evangelism strategy week or weekend gives youth an opportunity to develop a witnessing life-style. Learning through participation, not lecture, is emphasized. The four training sessions may take place in a retreat setting or in four nights at the local church. Youth discuss their spiritual experiences and how to share them with others. The sessions climax with youth actually sharing the story of Jesus' life and death with other young people.

Growth and outreach follow. Facets of this period include:

(1) the "touch ministry" in which adult leaders become involved in witness with youth;

(2) the "discipleship ministry" in which leaders assist in evangelism and discipleship training emphasizing personal commitment and continuing witness involvement. This helps youth grow in personal relationship with God and ability to reach out to the world through a witnessing life-style;

(3) the "sharing ministry" in which every young person is encouraged to consistently participate. There is no doubt this is what God really wants for youth.

And there is no doubt that if adults can channel the energies of youth, the experiments of youth, into Christian outreach and ministry, the world will become a better, more Christ-like place in only a few generations.

7

Evangelism— Proclamation to the Masses

~~~~~~

Therefore since we have this ministry, as we received mercy, we do not lose heart, but we have renounced the things hidden because of shame, not walking in craftiness or adulterating the word of God, but by the manifestation of truth commending ourselves to every man's conscience in the sight of God. And even if our gospel is veiled, it is veiled to those who are perishing, in whose case the god of this world has blinded the minds of the unbelieving, that they might not see the light of the gospel of the glory of Christ, who is the image of God. For we do not preach ourselves but Christ Jesus as Lord, and ourselves as your bond-servants for Jesus' sake. For God, who said, "Light shall shine out of darkness," is the One who has shone in our hearts to give the light of the knowledge of the glory of God in the face of Christ (2 Cor. 4:1–6).

7

Prologue

When I was growing up, we had a cowboy preacher in our home church. He had less than a fifth-grade education, but he was intelligent and full of zeal. He'd memorized the Bible, and he was an excellent preacher. He grew the church from a mission to an attendance of 200-250 each Sunday.

It was in this church, in the days of World War II, that I came under great conviction about my life.

Our family was poor; we had nothing. All we children worked. I'd earned my own money since I was thirteen or fourteen. I handled it well, saving some along, because I wanted to go to college.

After graduation from high school, I sold some cows I had and, armed with the promise of a job at college, I left home. The college didn't have a job for me, however, and I lost everything. I was pretty discouraged.

I came home and found a job working for a man who owned a lucrative auto supply store. Over the next months, he came to like me. Because he had no sons, he offered me a chance to become his "son" in an inheritance relationship. When he died, I would take over his business.

His bank account, I knew, totaled more than a quarter of a million dollars; if I went with him and kept my good senses, I knew I could be a millionaire someday. Everything I'd ever dreamed about as a kid was being handed to me. It was really tempting.

But I knew the hand of God was on me.

I kept fighting it, though.

I was rebelling. I had determined God had the right to save my soul—that was his business. But I was going to run my own life. I had never been taught the concept of Lordship; my background was filled with the negatives: don't smoke, don't drink, don't have sex, etc.

We were having a revival and the church was experiencing some tremendous spiritual blessings. I was miserable.

Dad was going, and he wanted me to go with him; but I didn't enjoy it. Finally, I decided I had to settle things.

I made an appointment to talk to the preacher; when I got off work at the auto store, I went to the church. The preacher took me into the back, into one of the primary rooms, where we sat in those little bitty chairs.

He locked the door. I guess he thought I was going to run away.

"Okay, Bill," he said to me, "what do you want to tell me?"

"Pastor, I'm miserable. Maybe I need to think about rededicating my life."

Evidently he knew more about what I was feeling than I did. He replied, "I think there's more to it than that. God is trying to deal with you about you doing something for him."

I said, "Well, if you think I'm going to preach, you're out of your head."

He was a gentle, kind man. He didn't get angry; he just suggested we pray. But I wasn't going to be forced to do anything.

"I'm not going to," I said.

"Listen, Bill," he said firmly. "You came here for a purpose. I'm not going to waste time with you. If you

can't pray about your problems, at least you can thank God for what he's done for you. Can't you get up the courage to do that?"

I knew I'd make a fool of myself, but I wanted to get him off my back. I started mumbling out some stuff. But suddenly I shouted, "Lord, if you want me to preach, I'll preach."

I didn't really have any control over it.

Right there I went into an emotional tizzy; I cried and squalled and carried on.

I'm not an emotional person; I'm basically timid, reserved. I may get tears in my eyes when something touches me, but I don't cry. I did that day. Amazingly, I had an inner peace I had not known for more than a year.

I knew my course; there was no doubt about it. I was to preach. He touched me . . . I had registered my decision in life's ultimate choice.

7

Evangelism — Proclamation to the Masses

With the increased emphasis on personal, confrontational witness, some religious leaders have begun to question the effectiveness of public proclamation. They reason that in today's impersonal society, mass preaching is dated; direct one-to-one encounters are the only way to win the world, they say.

But nothing could be further from the truth. Personal, friend-to-friend, human being-to-human being contact is necessary. But the New Testament example of public proclamation set for us by men such as Paul and Peter and carried on by generations of evangelists and preachers from John Wesley to Billy Sunday is still a valid, viable method of reaching people.

Preaching remains, in fact, an essential ingredient in all evangelism theory.

Paul said to the church at Corinth, "Woe is me if I preach not the gospel." Paul's divine call has been repeated again and again in history. It is still being repeated today, for the New Testament method—while hardly sacred in itself—has yet to be replaced as one important means of communicating the message of salvation to the multitudes who need to hear of Jesus.

In New Testament times, much public proclamation took place in the synagogue. At other times it occurred in the marketplace, in open-air theaters, on hillsides away from the crowded towns and villages.

History records public proclamation taking place in such "unholy" locations as prisons, theaters, town squares, tents, sports arenas, as well as giant cathedrals. Billy Sunday built massive auditoriums with "collapsible walls" for his public proclamation; Billy Graham has spoken in football stadiums and on Wall Street in New York City.

Though much public proclamation is still conducted in public areas from city coliseums to athletic field houses, most of the public proclamation of the gospel today occurs in the hundreds of churches in the United States.

Evangelists, therefore, classify most public proclamation by the nature of its outreach and the location in which it is held. The three types are:

1. the traditional worship service during which a preacher delivers a sermon that attempts to move those in the congregation without a saving belief in Jesus into a right relationship with the Savior;

2. a revival, usually held two or three times a year, which has a special "visiting evangelist" to speak and which draws, if the congregation is successful in its promotion and preparation, numbers of people who do not usually attend the local church;

3. a crusade which is a revival wherein several churches work cooperatively to canvass a district or area of the city and/or county for a greater outreach than could be done if the churches worked alone.

Each type of public proclamation has had success in reaching people for Jesus, especially when men and women of the community reach out boldly to touch the lives of neighbors and friends, and when the person who speaks understands the risks of evangelism but refuses to retreat from his intention to penetrate society with the message of salvation and judgment.

Each type of public proclamation also has its place in the local church, for no program of evangelism is complete without individual and cooperative efforts by churches to win the world for Jesus Christ.

But public proclamation is not easy evangelism.

Easy evangelism does not make a strong, stalwart church, only an easy religion which leads to a trouble-filled, weak church. The evangelism event, therefore, whether revival or crusade, costs the congregation—in time, effort and money.

A series of services, ill-thought through and poorly prepared, is unsatisfactory. There needs to be a time of preparation for each event plus an extensive effort at follow-up. Without such work, no revival, crusade or preaching service will provide much long-term benefit for the church or the people involved, and certainly not for the few who come to hear.

But if the proclamation is carried out in proper order, the community will respond with a joyous celebration of the depth and breadth of the Christian experience.

Every church regularly schedules preaching services. Most of the audience for such services—95 to 98 percent—are persons who are already members of that church. Yet that does not preclude the possibility of a preaching service evangelizing the small number in the congregation who are not Christians.

The worship serves most of the congregation as a strengthening experience that prepares individuals to enter the world and live for Christ. Spiritually, it is the Christians' source of power for another week's encounter with non-Christians, a time of fellowship and nearness to God and Jesus.

But it can also be a time when Christians express what God has done in their lives; their testimony can be an openly programed part of the service, or it can be subtle as each worshiper participates fully in the worship activities.

No service should end without a public invitation, when any who have been convicted of the truth of Christ are challenged to come forward and make public their decision to stand for Christ. At such a time new Christians and old Christians share the joy of fellowship and the meaning of the Christian life in a unique corporate experience.

As Euelpistus responded to the prefect who asked, "And what are you?" so the congregation answers in the hymn of invitation, "I too am a Christian, having been set at liberty by Christ."

Occasionally each church wants to have a special time of evangelistic emphasis in which the congregation is challenged to renew its experience with Jesus and to help bring others into that same saving relationship. The event is most often called a revival. Some refer to such times as an opportunity to "revive the saints." The congregation faced with heightened awareness of the lost condition of its community redoubles its prayer and witness efforts. Even if no new converts join the church, the occasion of a revival can bring new life to a tired congregation.

Noted evangelists from Spurgeon to Gypsy Smith have admitted the importance of a revival being a time for refreshing the believers as well as reaching the unsaved. Of course, reaching the unsaved is a primary objective of the revival. It is a time for calling men and women into a confrontation with Jesus, of demanding a decision before the hourglass sand runs out.

If the revival has as its central intent the task of bringing people to God, if it has the special flavor and power of the Holy Spirit, if it magnifies our Lord above all else, it will result in people who have a conversion experience as well as church members with a new sense of discipleship.

Revivals are not for growing memberships, budgets and buildings, but to build worship, discover the presence of Jesus, expand fellowship, create an atmosphere of love and concern that is necessary for a church to light its community.

If stronger stewardship results, well and good. Usually it is one of the benefits of a revival. If the congregation grows in number, excellent. That, too, happens when revivals take hold. But the most important aspect is that through public proclamation, people are moved to an awareness of their individual responsibility: to accept Jesus or reject him; to live for Jesus or to live against his will.

The third type of public proclamation, a crusade or unified campaign of several churches (as in a parish or association), involves the same procedures but even greater preparation than a local church revival. The most successful crusades are often a year or more in planning.

But like the local revival, they are the church's way of saying to the community, "We are interested in you." The crusade, like the revival, declares that the church is alive and well; that something is happening among its members that involves the world. A revival or a crusade or any public proclamation asks all outsiders, "Won't you come into the family of God?"

Without public proclamation of the gospel, many people would never hear of Jesus Christ. But without proper preparation, the effort of public proclamation is usually wasted. Evangelist Charles Finney used to say, "Revivals have to be worked up as well as prayed down." Weeks of preparation must be spent before the actual event. Prayer is the essential beginning; naturally, publicity follows.

A local church or several churches planning a crusade should kick off the event with a weekend of renewal evangelism. The renewal experience sharpens the sensitive, spiritual relationship of the local church member toward Jesus Christ; it focuses on individual responsibility to minister to those who do not know the Lord.

Following the renewal weekend, the congregation—with a new zeal for Christ—should be equipped for their roles in the revival. One method is to hold a lay evangelism school, which has been an amazingly successful way to prepare lay people by giving them tools for witness and confidence in their ability to make evangelism their life-style.

Certainly the church and community should prepare organizationally as well as spiritually. Committees involving as many people as possible should be elected. From inception of idea to the moment the event ends—and beyond—total involvement of the membership is absolutely necessary. The more involved, the more reached.

An area-wide crusade is different from a local church revival in three basic aspects. At the same time it has a simpler focus than a local church revival. Its only purpose is to preach Christ and him crucified. There will be many side effects but only one simple purpose.

First, it has a freshness about it because it does not take place in an established, preprogramed organization. Because it is a cooperative effort between churches of several denominations in a local community, a completely new organization has to be formed through which the preparation for, participation in, and follow-through of the event can take place. This gives the Spirit of God an opportunity to work from a new beginning in a community.

Second, it provides neutral ground for those who do not know Christ as personal Savior to hear the gospel. In most cases that ground is also familiar ground. The use of public facilities that non-Christians are accustomed to frequenting is a great asset in an area-wide crusade. Many people would never darken the door of a church building but will attend a religious event in a public facility such as a gymnasium, stadium, etc.

Third, the involvement of multitudes of laity is possible because much work must be done for such a gigantic event in a local area. The key to an area-wide crusade is the involvement of as many people as possible in all phases of preparation, participation, and follow-through. The involvement of multitudes gives the opportunity for many individual channels through which God can work in a local community. This, of course, is one of the major factors in the success of area-wide crusades. Fellowship among the local Christians who have usually been divided by denomination and church can grow and flourish during an area-wide crusade. The kingdom of God benefits when his vineyard grows.

For the crusade many churches turn to a vocational evangelist. There are several reasons for doing so. As an outsider, the vocational evangelist can speak in terms and ways different from those a congregation hears weekly. The difference does not necessarily mean better communication but rather that his voice and manner of expression might add insight.

Also, vocational evangelists give a special dimension to the event. Although the entire church should engage in evangelism, God calls and equips some members to be vocational evangelists. They have an unusual ability to make the gospel plain and to lead people to embrace it.

A sincere vocational evangelist is an asset to the whole ministry. These men are effective in total evangelism, leading churches into deeper, growing, spiritual experiences as they publicly touch the heart and life of the community.

Finally, the church planning a revival or crusade should concentrate on the lostness of its community, the uniqueness of Christ, the power of faith and the insight of God's purpose for humankind.

At all times, church members should remember that the source of any public proclamation's power is the risen Lord. His life and death are the Good News that gives strength to the church's efforts and promise to the public proclamation of hope and love that is Jesus Christ.

8

Evangelism and Disciple-making

But God, being rich in mercy, because of His great love with which He loved us, even when we were dead in our transgressions, made us alive together with Christ (by grace you have been saved), and raised us up with Him, and seated us with Him in the heavenly places, in Christ Jesus, in order that in the ages to come He might show the surpassing riches of His grace in kindness toward us in Christ Jesus. For by grace you have been saved through faith; and that not of yourselves, it is the gift of God; not as a result of works, that no one should boast. For we are His workmanship, created in Christ Jesus for good works, which God prepared beforehand, that we should walk in them (Eph. 2:4–10).

8

Prologue

I guess discipleship really became a clear concept for me when I was a teen-ager. I'd committed myself to preach, and my pastor helped me understand that my personal, one-to-one relationships with people were often as important as standing in the pulpit, preaching to people to get things done.

One of the men in our church in Corpus Christi, a fellow in the navy, also taught me about discipleship. He showed us youth a deep love and concern for people; he helped us understand Christian responsibility and Christian witness.

These two men set me on a pattern of Christian expression that has lasted my whole life. But they also caused me to think about the way many church members are. I realized how many church people love the church, feel an obligation to keep its doors open, yet are not really committed to the concepts of discipleship. They never develop a relationship to Christ that stretches to the limits of openness and witness. But seeing these two men made me appreciate the ones who go deeper into the sort of life Christ commands.

I remember a deacon in my church at Happy.

He was about fifty-five years old, a very wealthy man; he came out of a family that had nothing. He didn't have much education but he had a keen mind. And he was successful.

He put himself into whatever he did—business, play, church.

He was a student of the Bible, a Sunday school teacher, an active witness at home, at work, wherever he went. He didn't push himself on people, but he was unashamed to speak what he knew the Bible had to say.

That man cared for people; he showed his concern in his relationships with others. His life was evidence of his Christian dedication.

I've heard people say of him, "You know, there goes a great man, a wonderful Christian."

He had that kind of reputation, I think, because his life overflowed with his sense of discipleship. He was a sample in God's showcase.

8

Evangelism and Disciple-making

Lewis Abbott, pastor of a north Georgia church, believes most Christians "are not functioning in society as the Lord outlines it. The Lordship of Christ is being stifled." He has set about remedying that condition.

More than two hundred of his church's members have or are now taking intensive training in a one-year-long discipleship course that emphasizes the ministry and responsibilities of every Christian and deemphasizes the gap between the clergy and laity.

"Such a gap," says Abbott, "prevents the church from realizing the 'body of Christ' concept. What we've tried to do is assure a spiritual climate and tone for the church, and in that climate, work within the institution."

Abbott stresses to each of his members that "God has a ministry for you." And, as a result, forty-three different ministries have been established by church members, working on their own initiatives.

"These ministries, and the involvement of our members in them," Abbot says, "has been due to acceptance of the 'lifestyle evangelism' concept and the ability of those involved to recognize a 'Lordship of Christ' discipleship in their lives."

Making disciples today is a popular church pastime. But doing so with the effectiveness of a Lewis Abbott is altogether too rare.

In fact, we have many church members, but few real disciples. Church leaders, meanwhile, voice growing concern about uncommitted members. Statistics indicate fewer than half of those belonging to churches actually attend and regularly participate in activities.

Even fewer carry the load of church work. Church rolls swell, but the names on them are faceless; contentment replaces challenge.

"The church was founded to promote spiritual revolution," says Dean Inge. "Instead, it has almost strangled it."

Adds Christian philosopher Elton Trueblood, "We are so familiar with and hardened to the story that it is easy for us to forget how explosive and truly revolutionary faith was in Mediterranean beginnings. Our temper is so different that we hardly understand what the New Testament writers are saying. Once the church was a brave and revolutionary fellowship changing the course of history by the introduction of disturbing ideas. Today it is a place where people go and sit on comfortable benches waiting patiently until time to go home to their Sunday dinners."

And Robert Coleman, professor of evangelism, says, "When his [Christ's] plan is reflected upon, the basic philosophy is so different from the modern church that its implications are nothing less than revoluntionary."

Obviously, the feverish and frustrating activities and programs of most of our churches are not producing the revolutionaries whose likeness is to Christ.

But why is this? Why are we not down to the business of maturing born-again Christians into the sort of activist disciples Christ intended them to be? For, indeed, that is the command of Christ.

Barry St. Clair, a youthful evangelist with the Southern Baptist Convention, observes that "it is significant Jesus said, 'Make disciples,' instead of 'Make decisions,' or merely, 'Preach the Gospel.'

"It is significant because the purpose of making disciples is to lead people into a personal, intimate, and mature relationship with God through Jesus Christ.

"Making disciples," St. Clair continues, "means not only bringing a person into an initial relationship with Christ, but bringing that person to be conformed into the very image of Jesus Christ Himself."

The eminent scholar, Marcus Dodds, adds that "if we would be Christ's followers, we must be prepared to make his experience ours; his work, our work; his person, our chief joy." Yet, many Christians stop after the initial experience. Believing their sins to be forgiven, their place in the family of God assured, they drift lazily into an ecclesiastical ennui that promotes the institution, rather than the individual; that stresses membership, rather than discipleship.

Merely being on a church roll does not make one a true disciple. New Testament discipleship involves much more than just attending church; it demands a costly, self-sacrificing followership: obedience to, recognition of authority of, and submission to the teachings of Christ. Dedication and commitment are implicit.

Where churches do not confront their members with this commitment, this dedication, disenchantment and discontent develop. In many cases, para-church groups who do challenge Christians to roles of active discipleship siphon off members.

Sometimes, unwittingly, churches can also stress discipleship too heavily. There are dangers in myopic discipleship, the sort of Bible study that becomes an end in itself, not a process that carries the believer along the footsteps of Christ. Some, in fact, have become so enmeshed in the principles they forget the actual practice: witnessing, in word and deed, Jesus Christ to bring those who do not know him into a personal relationship with God through him.

Discipleship study, plainly, can be a cop-out, an escape from serious participation in the acts of discipleship. Disciples, after all, are not mass-produced, but individually shaped by God's Spirit and responsible to his guidance.

Nevertheless, if discipleship follows the true biblical pattern, it provides a depth and meaning that will color every aspect of living, tinting it in hues of the woman at the well, the tenth leper, the sacrifice of the cross.

For when Christ becomes Lord, a person's values and attitudes change. Actions are molded by the life-gaining experience of conversion. Each day becomes an opportunity for evangelism.

W. Maxfield Garrott, long-time missionary of the Southern Baptist Foreign Mission Board, has written: "Neglected axioms, things everyone takes for granted and no one seems to take seriously, lie at the foundation of Jesus' creation of the yeastly nucleus of a world-changing force. Among them are these principles:

1. That a few workers thoroughly trained are more effective than many superficially trained. *The principle of concentration.*
2. That the essential training for Christian leadership is character training. *The principle of personality.*
3. That the most potent instrument of character training is personal association. *The principle of contact.*
4. That characteristic training is most thorough and effective when it is carried out under life conditions. *The principle of reality.*

Simply put, Garrott is saying we know much about disciple-ship, but we have done little to apply our knowledge to our existence in the world.

But if we are to win the world, we must begin to turn Christian novices into Christian disciples. And, as Walter Henricksen of the Navigators organization says, "We must capture Jesus' vision of 'reaching the world through the use of multiplying disciples.' All he said pulsates that vision culminating in the Great Commission."

Echoes evangelist John Havlik, "Our responsibility is evangelizing the pagans and discipling the saints."

This is the essence of all the church has to do today. Clearly, the responsibility of the church is to teach and train, to build and develop Christian disciples who, in their everyday experiences, become the evangelistic followers of Jesus Christ that New Testament writings describe.

For the ultimate purpose of leading people into a personal, intimate, mature discipleship is to involve the people of God in the process, the priorities, the patterns of evangelistic living.

In true Christian discipleship, the life-styles of Christians are so changed they come to grips with the claims of Christ and share those claims with others.

The inevitable result of the discipling process is natural witnessing, the uninhibited sharing of Christ from the overflow of one's personal commitment to him. New designs for living emerge, reflecting a way of life that verbally and physically expresses the joy and peace and love of the Son of man.

Because the Christian journey is one of understanding discipleship, the process of making disciples must become a priority for the churches. Instilling into the mind of the church the concern of Christ, both for those who are part of his "body on earth" and those who are separated from it, is a command too long neglected. Evangelistic zeal without discipleship is froth, a shallow and self-effacing style of witness.

Responsible evangelism, however, includes discipleship; Christians reproduce other Christians, mature other Christians.

Without an emphasis on discipleship, the church has a luke-warm center and a frosty fringe. But by keying on the center, weaving those members who express initial concern into the discipleship fabric, the edges will gradually become part of the cloth, too. And the church will experience a new aware-ness of life-style evangelism.

Excitement evident in the life of the church will spill over. People filled with a keen spiritual maturity will offer that same growth experience to others.

And the church in these years will literally conform to the image and eternal purpose of Jesus Christ. It will be God's showcase and we will be the samples.

9

Evangelism—
Overwhelmed by Opinions

Therefore if any man is in Christ, he is a new creature; the old
things passed away; behold, new things have come. Now all
these things are from God, who reconciled us to Himself through
Christ, and gave us the ministry of reconciliation, namely,
that God was in Christ reconciling the world to Himself, not
counting their trespasses against them, and He has committed to us
the word of reconciliation. Therefore, we are ambassadors
for Christ, as though God were entreating through us; we beg you
on behalf of Christ, be reconciled to God. He made Him who
knew no sin to be sin on our behalf, that we might become the
righteousness of God in Him (2 Cor. 5:17–21).

9

Prologue

I enjoyed my seminary studies. One course of interest was the one on evangelism. Scriptures were memorized, concern generated about the people outside of Christ, and a few methods of soul winning were taught.

However, about all I really knew of evangelism was what I learned from this course and some past experiences. These involved my own experiences in youth-led revivals and what was learned from visiting speakers in revivals. My pastors taught me some things from their practices and expressed concepts.

Frankly, all these did not give me adequate foundation or preparation for practicing evangelism as a pastor. So, when I graduated from seminary my thinking regarding evangelism was in a state of flux. It was pliable and began to show signs of change.

Talking to friends, doing some reading, I soon discovered there were about as many philosophies of evangelism as there were church leaders. Evidence began to indicate there were not many really good concepts toward the matter.

The word evangelism *seemed to bear a negative connotation. Maybe it was from apparent Madison Avenue and manipulative methods. I got caught up in the negative thinking. Yet, there was that drive to be successful and need to keep a good personal record of church attendance and of baptisms.*

Moving from one church to another kept me searching for quick answers and methods and being influenced by these various philosophies of outreach.

How I longed for guidance which my studies through education should have provided. The desire for a solid philosophy of reaching people continued to gnaw at me.

In every spiritual quest which eventuated a deep renewal, I began reading everything I could get my hands on hoping to get some legitimate handles on evangelism. Everybody had his own method, his gimmick, or the process of a structure.

Finally, I began to study seriously Jesus' practice and expressions of concern for people. Then the New Testament began to speak to me in terms of what God really intended in reaching people. I discovered a new joy in developing sharing concepts with some of my people— and became unashamed in proclaiming that every Christian is a witness.

My regret was I learned so late the realistic approach of New Testament evangelism for solid church growth. But when it became real, it became a time of action. I could not be bothered about what everybody thought of the matter or what the climate might be.

I had to do it!

9

Evangelism— Overwhelmed by Opinions

The bookshelves in the study of most pastors possess rows of "how to" works related to evangelism. Some are deep. Some are shallow. They explain every conceivable opinion of evangelism and outreach. They come from every segment of the religious society. So, what is a pastor to do? As he begins to share with his lay people, what are they to do? These extremes normally come to bear upon the mind-set of the pastor or the mind-set of the people of the church.

Two leading concepts of evangelism are mass evangelism and personal evangelism. Mass evangelism includes a wide variety of mass media, crusades, etc. While the other is personal confrontation. Evangelism falls into these or between.

Too often the pastor or the church people become preoccupied with the machinery and the programs of the church. Consequently, evangelism as reaching those outside of Christ does not build the church and fulfill the commission of our Lord.

A variety of opinions surface in religious subjectives liberal, hyperfundamental, charismatic, and a multitude of other expressions. Each vies for the attention of the leadership within the church. Each seeks to control the mind of the people who are involved. Mention of some of these should be noted.

Some subscribe to the syncretistic point of view which says that all religions have good, so let's mesh them. Surely, they are trying to satisfy man's needs. So, to become passionately involved in reaching a world for the Christian concept is no necessity.

D. T. Niles described a Hindu who would have a picture of Christ in the Hindu temple. I was reminded of that when I talked to a young college student from the Far East. By placing the picture of Christ in the Hindu temple satisfaction indicates the best of both worlds. The young college student from the Far East said, "I am of another religion, but if I am in America I will embrace Christianity. When I am home I will return to my traditional religion. That means I can accept both and they will satisy the needs of the people where I am."

He completely missed the entire point of what the Christian message has to say. Jesus declared, "I am the Way, the Truth, and the Life." There is no syncretistic view. There is only one way!

Some would say, "Let's educate the world. Let's develop a better life existence for our world. We must clean up the environment. Let us set better patterns of life so the people will consider reconciliation with each other." These utopian views are consistently academic.

Added to that others say, "What we must do in our time is speak to the contemporary existential situation—which issues change and revolution. Traditional concepts as heaven and hell should have no place in evangelism for today." With evangelism the sense of urgency, "Pluck the brands from the burning," and proclaiming this to the outsider are gone. "Fit the place of serious contemporary issues," they say. Contemporary evangelism in their concept speaks only to that which is happening externally.

Past and present voices are pleading acquiescence, "Let God win the world." William Carey was a young man on fire to spread the Good News. At a meeting with other ministers he expressed his profound concern regarding sharing the Good News. The presiding officer countered, "Sit down young man. When God is pleased to convert the heathen he will do it without your aid or mine."

Some equate evangelism with revivalism, and rejecting revivalism reject any evangelism through prejudice. Consequently, evangelism has been confused with revivalism. The pattern which many evangelists use traditionally took shape in the nineteenth century and subsequently.

Most who reject revivalism do so through rather unpleasant experiences in childhood in unethical evangelistic services. We are tempted to search for gimmicks to attract crowds and then excite the people to an emotional frenzy. But when the hangover is gone the question is consistently asked, "What then?"

Perhaps we have depended upon Madison Avenue evangelism. Plans and practices, rallies and campaigns, sermons and testimonies, big meetings, little meetings, all must consistently be examined in the whole presentation of the gospel. Again the question arises, "Are these of God?" If so, let them stand.

Dependence upon emotional high excitement of frenetic and sometimes weird activity of the snakehandlers or the "high rollers" often turns off the more sensitive nature of some. Consequently, this type of evangelism is rejected.

Instant success is the name of the game. We would like to reach on the shelves and pull out a quick evangelism, mix a little of this and a little of that, spread it to the church and expect a great harvest. We want instant success in revivals and easy training schools for the laity. All these conspire to bring a poor harvest.

I pastored in the Panhandle of Texas and remember the great grain harvest season. Those who prepared the seedbeds for sowing and cultivated them harvested great and mighty crops. But God had to supply the rain. On the other hand those who did not prepare well did not reap good crops, rain or no rain.

It seems that many of our church leaders are like the farmer who planted little. When the farmer suddenly realized it was time for the harvest, he hired a fantastic crew with a magnificent harvest machine. The machine had a racing stripe on the side and was quite colorful. The harvester came to the fields, rushed across them and stirred up the dust. When he was gone the harvest was sparce—little to show for the effort.

Pastor-evangelist Leslie Woodson says, "No church can effectively do the job of bringing them to Christ by simply conducting one revival each year. Often this kind of church has slipped into the life of least resistance and would be shocked and horrified if such a meeting would actually become a revival."

Others say, "We would just love the people. When they know we love them they will come to us. We do not have to go to them." This is an extreme. Some think that by being good and saying nice things will bring the world to them. This attitude ignores the very fact that Jesus said, "As ye go, you make disciples." There is no place in the New Testament where he mentioned they would come to the believer.

One great extreme related to evangelism is harsh, cold orthodoxy. The Pharisees, Sadducees, and Herodians were expressive of some of the modern religionists. Someone classified the Pharisees as the fundamentalists, the Sadducees as the liberals, and the Herodians as the religious politicans. In any of these three extremes several things could happen related to the matter of concerns in evangelism.

Concentration upon theological correctness, a highly motivated orthodox theology, is nothing more than a way of escape from getting into the battle of the world which does not know Jesus Christ. It is much easier to split hairs and hunt heresies. This keeps Christians too busy to evangelize.

On the other hand some are given to the practice of evangelism that brings more zeal than wisdom to the task. Some techniques which claim compassion treat persons as things and manipulate human personality. This approach centers on man's abilities rather than God's power. Some have taken the purely negative attitude, acutely aware of the dangers and improprieties into which evangelism could fall. They are quite vocal about the kind of evangelism that they don't believe in but not so articulate about the kind they do.

Having been a pastor for a long time and now in denominational service, I am impressed that programs are thought to be the answer to our total evangelistic needs. Here we are frantically calling for and attending meetings and clinics, racing off to other churches, denominations and church groups who seem to be really engaged in evangelism, looking for the panacea. Yet the world is still lost and is becoming even more lost as the population explodes each day. Too often our concept is to invent a plan rather than discover God's strategy. Plans and methods may well become our masters. When they do, they are ugly and tyrannical. An evangelism system of a purely program nature indicates, "Here are the ways to do it. No other will do." Emphasis upon such programs of evangelism may be more upon the programs themselves than upon Christ.

Evangelist John Havlik expresses the problem which some feel when he declared, "God is on the side of the church or denomination that has the most dollars, best methods, nicest facilities, etc."

Charismatics with Pentecostal concepts think differently than some in certain areas of evangelism. While a great emphasis upon the Holy Spirit is commendable, the emphasis upon the gifts of the Holy Spirit is overbalanced against the emphasis of the giver. Preaching a different gospel from the gospel of Christ is the theme. Charismatics claim more good news about gifts and not as much good news about Jesus Christ. It is an evangelism which feeds on itself and does not fulfill the commission that Jesus Christ has declared.

Recently in conversation a man said, "What we need is a grand movement of God like Finney and Whitefield and the masters of old." He was relating that he liked the great "old time religion." If one speaks of the "old time religion" as the same spiritual commitment and evangelistic passion of Finney, Whitefield, and Moody, that is worthy. Yet we become caught up in expressing an unusual desire for the "good old days" and lustily sing "Give Me That Old Time Religion." The purpose verbalizes the desire for a fresh breath of God's moving power. If this were taken literally, God's refreshing presence would be welcomed with precious joy in today's desert of circumstances.

On the other hand, some aspects of the "old time religion" are not appropriate as they perhaps were during the latter 1800s—such as mouth frothing, tying to stakes, "being slain in the Spirit." Expression of emotional frenzy is not the brand of evangelism identified with the New Testament practice. But old patterns and methods which stand the test of circumstances and time are worthy of consideration. Unless these come under careful scrutiny and receive new breaths of the Spirit they cannot be classified as hopeful expressions of work.

A person asked recently, "What is wrong with old techniques?" The answer is "Nothing, if they are of God." But God is not limited to time or circumstances. He may choose to step into our culture with creative and innovative new concepts of witness. He knows in this country our great cities are melting pots of all peoples. Much of community life is cosmopolitan.

To talk of the "old time religion" and the "old techniques" and the old methods "which were truly good for Paul and

Silas"—let's examine them honestly. They had a commitment, and in the power of the Holy Spirit, they walked into danger and never looked back. They faced the governments, communities, and the pagan witness of their time. Yet God strengthened them and blessed them.

The preceding discussion has only touched on some of the issues which frustrate today's pastor and congregation as they consider true concepts of evangelism. Methods of hope, grasping for the real thing, are only like the search for the Holy Grail, finding nothing but emptiness in clasping hands, and "going down dusty roads and finding no water."

The person who would practice true evangelism is not limited to a simple method, plan, or program! His announcement that Jesus Christ came to the world as the Savior, Life, Giver, and Victor over death is the theme. He must also know and declare Jesus as Lord. That declaration is an evangelism which changes the world. It develops ministries that touch people. It states an obvious reality of God for the good of man.

Therefore, the laity and the ministry must link their hands together, put their arms around each other, and step into the secular situation seriously confronting man in his depths while walking within man's systems.We must do whatever is necessary to change the circumstances by the grace of God. We must faithfully rest in the Lord in order to effectively transmit the Good News.

Responsibility for reaching the outsider must return to the heart of the church. Placement of it there demands a sense of urgency and the recognition of the centrality of evangelism to the church. If lost, the church loses the right of continuing existence. Evangelism is the proclamation of the Good News. God is in Christ reconciling the world to himself through his church.

Look to the New Testament for the happy medium of it all.

Dare not question. First-century Christians had their problems. They were assailed on every hand with all ideologies and philosophies. Yet, they met the need of people where they were. The people heeded because of the power of God in their midst. They did it naturally and because of the conviction that this was the work and the will of the Father. They knew the power of Jesus Christ in their lives! Whatever else they were, they were evangelists, speaking and sharing the Good News.

It is revolutionary. Being revolutionary pays no attention to the opinions of men and what they think in terms of evangelism. Our chief end is evangelism—to glorify God. The Scripture is clear, "Do all for the glory of God."

Ras Robinson, a layperson in Fort Worth, Texas, tells how seeking office space he visited a builder. Somehow he was unable to leave that builder without verbal witness which led to the man's open expression of his commitment to Jesus Christ. It was natural and spontaneous. That is evangelism, no matter what anyone thinks and whatever one may declare in opinions, philosophy, and ideology. The doing of it is the reality. It is natural in Christ, by his power, through his will. Evangelism rejects our preoccupations with the frills. It calls for action!

10

Innovations and Change

Not that I have already obtained it, or have already become perfect, but I press on in order that I may lay hold of that for which also I was laid hold of by Christ Jesus. Brethren, I do not regard myself as having laid hold of it yet; but one thing I do; forgetting what lies behind and reaching forward to what lies ahead. I press on toward the goal for the prize of the upward call of God in Christ Jesus (Phil. 3:12–14).

10

Prologue

It was nothing unusual as a boy to hear from the pulpit that a fellow ought to get out and win souls. Sometimes as I heard these pulpit pounders cry, "Go, go out," I was never sure whether they were talking about themselves or us. But then occasionally it seemed this man behind the sacred desk was trying to say, "Go get another notch on your gun." I thought it was the thing to do.

Yet, when I would not do it I felt guilty. Sometimes I would respond to an invitation after the message and promise to do better. Often I would say I would be a witness, I would do my best to lead people to Christ. But I was scared. I never did quite get to it. Perhaps this was a reflection on some of the feelings later expressed in my ministry.

However, these feelings never did reject my sense of concern for people who were outside of Christ. After my commitment to preach the gospel I had an unusual zeal at the beginning. It was good to stand and declare the Good News. What an easy way to do it, because it meant facing many people instead of one. When I gave an invitation for a public decision some would respond and that was easy. But it was different going on a one-to-one basis.

On a one-to-one basis I learned I ought to use Scripture. Maybe some I had memorized or some I should have memorized but didn't know really well. That was a bother.

Eventually I was able to overcome some of these fears. I began to think in terms of my real responsibility which was to share the Good News with everybody.

After my ministerial education I was launched into a busy pastorate where I saw people as a part of Christian work. To me the soul-winning commitment day became important, so I would preach on the responsibility of us all to witness. Passionately the invitation would be given calling for people to "walk the aisle" to make a public commitment of that responsibility. Quite often many would do so. I thought, "Man, are we going to have a harvest! Are we really going to have many to be baptized!"

Unfortunately about the same number of baptisms occurred during the church year as did the last. Most of these came at my hand because as pastor I was the one literally witnessing. Such was the case in most of the churches that I pastored.

Because of this I never ceased to search for a vision— a vision that told me here was a world without Christ, that I needed to do something more than call for a commitment on a day for witness.

Why? Well, as a pastor I saw community corruption. I noted bad government. I counseled pregnant girls and talked to boys on drugs. I worked with dissipated parents. I saw the poor and understood them. I sympathized with the up and out, the poor and down. What was I to do?

Materials from the office of the state convention and from the national offices surely caught my time and my attention. But evangelism to be evangelism seemed to pull me into a preoccupation in which I was a victim and could not extricate myself. And I was busy doing all those things rather than the important thing of involvement.

The climate of evangelism was far off until I finally

came to the conclusion, "I am tired of all that which
crosses my desk. The hurt and ills of humanity are too
loud in my ears and pressing my flesh."

And so desperately I would do like a lot of other
pastors and run to this place and to that. I wrote for
all kinds of evangelism programs and materials until
finally I came to the conclusion that if I was really ready
to practice evangelism that I must not only do it but lead
my people and teach them. We walk together and we
share it in life-style—naturally, normally, sensitively with
those who hurt and those in desperation who cry, "I'm
lost!"

Well, maybe the pulpit pounder had something when
he said, "Go, go out!" In reflection, I am not really sure
he was saying, "Get another notch on your gun," but
rather the real thing is caring and sharing Jesus Christ.
I wanted to do it, and eventually I learned my people
wanted to do it, too.

10

Innovations and Change

The concern of the New Testament believers was for people. The message of Christ was directed to people. From person to person the Good News flowed. Their proclamation was church-related since they were the church. That redemptive relationship grew in spiritual maturity and community. Their community was not self-centered; they moved from it to share the gospel everywhere. They loved to proclaim it!

These early Christians expressed their evangelism with the realization that the Holy Spirit empowered them to share it inside and outside the group. What a boldness they had! With the Holy Spirit in charge they did not manipulate. Take a lesson from the spirit of these apostolic witnesses!

Using innovative methods in evangelism should not be a deterrent. Instead, every church and believer can be open-minded and life partners to "by all means win some." Denominational leader Dr. Albert McClellan amplified the problem by saying, "The need to find modern new methods for our evangelistic thrust is upon us. Man's basic spiritual needs have not changed. The rapidity of his physical and cultural environment has made him a person in a different set of circumstances from that of the past years. The processes of urbanization, industrialization, and communication underlie the scope of the problem."

Some of the problems are:

1. Impersonalism in which people seek anonymity because of a lack of personhood. They are non-related to others on a personal basis.
2. Massiveness describes the largeness of society with its overwhelming structures. This complexity of society with its mass communication and transportation necessitates our keeping together as a unit in a rapidly changing nation.
3. Mobility indicates the national transience which is much greater than a generation ago. Trends show a more rapid pace of mobility each day, which makes educational processes, living standards, and the total conditions of our day more complex.
4. Secularism with its emphasis upon materialism tends to draw from that which is spiritual to the extent that people forget their moorings and are thrown into the clutches of secularistic society.
5. Change is everywhere. The change in physical and cultural relationships has made man's physiological and psychological responses different today from those of our rural-oriented forefathers. Clusters of population are everywhere with changes in heterogeneous, social, and geographical relationships. Suddenly we are thrown into terms such as megalopolis (the urbanization of man), technopolis (the technological society); our cities become fractured, broken, and divided.

The problem becomes clear. Some churches where the percentage of converts comes from within the church family itself in response to these outside stimuli are withdrawing. This results in a low response to training opportunities to move outside the walls and make a definite impact upon those who do not know Christ.

The average church of today has not grasped the need of persons in an impersonal, massive, mobile, secular, and changing world. Those outside the church are characterized by alienation, social void, eclipse of community, and the loss of identity. The matter then becomes one of communication. Communication is the key to telling, announcing, and witnessing.

One problem in failing to reach the non-Christian is that our evangelistic mechanics and methods tend to serve the church's important organizational functions. The church is busy with itself—teaching itself, preaching to itself, receiving from itself, building for itself, and being pleased with itself. Sometimes church members get so involved in the organization of the church they have no time to know or cultivate the lost outsider.

An examination of the evangelistic program of many of our churches reveals that in our formal activities we provide few opportunities for contact with those outside of Christ. Meager exception would be the visitation programs, pastoral- or people-oriented. At the same time many of our people interact with the non-Christian but do not communicate their knowledge of Christ through commitment and involvement. Why is this?—failure to use innovative methods to bring people to know Jesus Christ.

Another reason why people do not move outside the walls to share is that we have taught "separation from the world" so much our people are really practicing it. When we say "go into the world" they have an uneasy feeling which leaves them bewildered. The weakness in communicating the message is not in the message itself but the communicators who project the message.

The proclaiming of the message is inside the church. We've been studying the message and that is all. We need to take the message to the non-Christian. The church that does not reach people for Christ is both biblically unfaithful and strategically short-sighted.

Let the church deal with the cultural society in which it lives and in which it survives. The church must define its responsibility. It must activate the empowering presence of the Holy Spirit and become witnesses of Jesus (Acts 1:8).

Although this chapter does not propose to settle all the implications of the failure to witness, some positive things need to be stated.

Reaching the outsider is the duty and the privilege of all Christians. Carefully evaluate the basic reason for service to Christ. It grows out of our theological commitment and our basic contact with men at the point of their basic needs.

Personal responsibility recognizes the changeless objective which is involved with a changeless message. This timeless message fits into any age in spite of rival philosophies and political tensions. The news of Christ must go everywhere and face the world's peculiarities at every point.

In a communicating process of the real message, the mandate is to recover the power of spiritual aggression by witnessing convincingly and positively. Be open and learn the lessons of the past. Take into account the realities of today's opportunities and find ways to communicate with man in his particular cultural environment.

More people must be saved than are now being saved. The mobility of Americans with its masses demand new ways. Proclamation through the media such as television, radio, cassette tapes, etc., offer excellent opportunities for communication. Such a modern approach to the application of New Testament concepts in dealing with the masses is a communicative process.

Evangelism must adapt its message and figures of speech, for it must say clearly, "Christ is the Good News to all!" Reaching people as did our New Testament forebears calls for a consistent practice. Opportunities for the church can stimulate and nurture small groups where a one-to-one evangelism is a possibility. Small groups for penetration and growth are absolutely necessary in our design. Homes for neighbor-to-neighbor and one-to-one relationships are examples. The church must "go out" rather than "call in." When a church gathers in fellowship it must also share the fellowship with those outside.

The priority of personal conversation is normal and a necessity. As we work in the marketplace, on our job, wherever we are in a life-style relationship, we can communicate clearly to those who do not know Christ. By sharing the Good News that he has worked in our lives we let them know Christ will also work in theirs. Be unafraid to develop new approaches which grow out of the old and find new methods in communicative processes which enable the individual to express his experience of what God is doing.

A New Testament way of life for our churches is reaching people and growing people in Christian maturity. Get back to the daring flexibility of the early believers. Such a flexibility may not be structured within organizational activity or a circumstantial structure of conduct built into the activity of the church. Keep in mind freedom for the presence of God to move in the life of an individual as well as in the life of the church.

Church growth specialist Donald McGavran has told of some molds on innovative methods in evangelism:

1. A one-to-one basis where one person in the family

     sometimes has to stand alone as a believer and witness within the family concept as against old cultural patterns.

2. The family movement to Christ where a progression is made from one family to another family expecting decisions made by that other family.

3. A people movement to Christ where joint decisions of many come to Christ as a result of an outpouring of the presence of God upon the lives of many who are together in a particular circumstance.

4. A multiplication in cities and villages of house churches, which is a viable possibility in our time if we are to innovatively reach out to touch people for Christ.

Believe God works in any age, at any time, on his terms and by his directions. He does it by reaching out to individuals, bringing them into fellowship and keeping them in fellowship for growth and responsibility.

Hope in the final triumph of Jesus Christ belongs to the essence of the Christian faith. What God did through the death and resurrection of his Son, he will complete at the end of time. This is our story and our message. Failure to use innovative methods in bringing hope to those who do not know Jesus Christ makes the believer fail miserably. The problem is inspiring churches and getting them involved in getting it done. If this is not done we shall feed on ourselves, baptize our own, and eventually die because there are no others beyond ourselves.

11

Equipped to Evangelize

Seeing that His divine power has granted to us everything pertaining to life and godliness, through the true knowledge of Him who called us by His own glory and excellence. For by these He has granted to us His precious and magnificent promises, in order that by them you might become partakers of the divine nature, having escaped the corruption that is in the world by lust. Now for this very reason also, applying all diligence, in your faith supply moral excellence, and in your moral excellence, knowledge; and in your knowledge, self-control, and in your self-control, perseverance, and in your perseverance, godliness; and in your godliness, brotherly kindness, and in your brotherly kindness, Christian love. For if these qualities are yours and are increasing, they render you neither useless nor unfruitful in the true knowledge of our Lord Jesus Christ. For he who lacks these qualities is blind or short-sighted, having forgotten his purification from former sins. Therefore, brethren, be all the more diligent to make certain about His calling and choosing you; for as long as you practice these things, you will never stumble; for in this way the entrance into the eternal kingdom of our Lord and Savior Jesus Christ will be abundantly supplied to you (2 Pet. 1:3–11).

11

Prologue

After seminary it did not take very long to discover that pastoring a church is an enjoyable but no easy task. I loved the pastorate. Yet sometimes I became so enmeshed in the administration, the business of church activities, routine but demanding duties that my time with God would be neglected.

The time came when there had to be time with God or my soul would be bare, my well would run dry, and my love relationship with him froth with despair. I made the decision that each day must have a period with him. In the last two pastorates especially, those moments in the study in the purely personal time when conversation with him took shape naturally, I grew in rejoicing and spiritual development.

Particularly after I discovered a new dimension in his Lordship did those times become more precious and guarded.

While in the pastorate with daily schedules and foreseeable routines, such a time with God in prayer, Bible study, and personal worship could be planned. I like to do that. Being alone with God was beautiful.

Then, when I was asked to become the director of evangelism for a state convention, one of the questions which plagued me was, "How can I have that time with God that is so enjoyable in normal pastoral schedules?"

It was not easy. I guess it is never really easy—making time for God!

Late-night denominational gatherings, constant travel, office demands, planning meetings—all conspired to keep me from daily experience with the Lord.

It bothered me greatly until it occurred to me I was responsible for my time. The discipline of my time was in my hands. No one else would control it for me. At that point I planned for such moments each day. Each was so delightful, for the presence of God ever pleased me with thankful joy. They were not set in certain times; only in the business of schedules must they claim their right. They did and it was great!

Moving into the national responsibility called for these moments to become more needful in my spiritual growth and relationship. They consistently reminded me of my own personal inadequacy, my inability to win my world by my own strength. They also serve to remind me of the work and witness of the Holy Spirit.

He indwells me and endows me with gifts of service which I alone do not possess. He gives me vitality, vision, and victory. My work would be nothing apart from his indwelling presence. He teaches me so much and develops my fellowship with the Father, makes Jesus more real, and makes me an evangelist.

11

Equipped to Evangelize

The question is often asked, "How do you really get ready to evangelize?" The usual answer is, "Go to a clinic, do a study, learn some Scriptures, use a tract." These may prove useful. However, a major aspect deleted from preparation to witness proves they are ineffective without the power and the presence of the Holy Spirit.

There is no doubt a person can be a witness, but I am not really sure of the power and the spontaneity of it. The reason lies within the spiritual condition of the majority of believers. The vast majority of believers appear quite satisfied with their spiritual condition. That is tragic! They are happy with the normal church life. They share only a minimum church life.

As an illustration, ask any average church member to pray. Some will do so loudly. Then ask him to go share his experience of conversion with another. He balks on the spot. Why? A variety of reasons may be mentioned: timidity, lack of knowledge of the Scriptures, insufficient know-how, and many others. Most likely this person has not had a deep, continuing and abiding relationship with Jesus Christ in a maturing Christian experience.

Churches often lose members and cannot find others because discipline in Christian maturity is neither taught nor expected. A large majority of children in Sunday school drift away from organized religion when they reach high school or college.

Most church members go on happily in their normal experience without seeing any results of witness. Sunday school teachers, church workers, sometimes staff members are busy about Christian activity and are never disturbed nor distressed that people are not coming to Christ through their witness. The argument is, "Of course we witness! We take up the tithe, sweep the church building, mow the grass, serve in an office in Sunday school class—that is our witness!" Yet this witness is not of the caliber called for in the New Testament. Jesus said, "You shall be My witnesses" (Acts 1:8). Specifically, he indicates they are to share that which they had experienced and knew in him. The Scriptures have much to say about our responsibilities. Jesus said to one of the churches, "Thou sayest, I am rich, and increased with goods, and have need of nothing; and knowest not thou art wretched" (Rev. 3:17, KJV). Spiritual poverty is quite evident. That church was not a strong, winning witness.

The Christian who charges into his work faces battle with the evil one. He must be prepared spiritually to be a winning witness. Paul declared to Timothy, "Thou therefore endure hardness, as a good soldier of Jesus Christ. No man that warreth entangleth himself with the affairs of this life; that he may please him who hath chosen him to be a soldier" (2 Tim. 2:3–4, KJV). Spiritual preparation for witness is a necessity. The point is to be placed in a position of greater usefulness and effectiveness.

Personal witnessing power in a life-style comes from being with God. John wrote, "What we have heard, what we have seen with our eyes, what we beheld and our hands handled

. . . we proclaim to you also" (1 John 1:1). The apostle said that power in personal sharing came from having been with God. Your personal life must be prepared to become the effective servant in a life-style relationship. The work you do significantly takes on new meaning when you have been with God.

Spending time with God burns evangelism in the soul and puts action in life. Being with Christ you have the same mind, and catch his vision. He saw the world. He knew his way to people was in the multiplication of disciples.

Note what may be learned from being with God:

1. You discover the mind of Christ. That indicates the importance of personal knowledge and a personal relationship with mutual confidence and trust. Time with God brings the risk of being fully involved with Christ. If you are not willing to move to that relationship, then you will be like the subnormal Christian whose witness is shallow and meager.

2. Being with God develops an understanding of his love for his people. Paul wrote to the Roman church, "And hope does not disappoint; because the love of God has been poured out within our hearts through the Holy Spirit who was given us" (Rom. 5:5). God's love is real. Human love is real. The fact he gave his only Son for the world is an indication of a love relationship. Being with God understands the depth of that love.

3. One of the things you learn from God is the knowledge of self. That knowledge reveals you may be entrapped with sin. An independent spirit is dangerous. Wrong attitudes are destructive. The

only answer to self is the discovery of the Lordship of Jesus Christ. When his lordship begins to
take shape the self-life begins to be molded into
the fullness of his will.

4. One cannot spend much time with Jesus without
the desire to be disciplined in the fullness of the
the Father's will. We can only rely on God en-
dowing us with the power to do his will. The example of Christ compels us in the fullness of his
will to faithfully do whatever is necessary to accomplish his desires in our lives. There is no
doubt the will of God according to the Scriptures
is to witness and to share the glory of our Father.

George Whitefield is credited with saying, "Oh, Lord, give
me souls or take my soul." Someone reported after Whitefield
once prayed, "He went to the devil's fair and took more than
a thousand souls out of the claw of the lion in a single day."
The evangelist once declared, "Having been with God he
knew what the will of God was in his life to share the Good
News."

Spiritual equipment for evangelism is a daily relationship to
God and a continuing indwelling power of the Holy Spirit.

Personal disciplines have proved to thousands a more adequate quality and growth in being a witness.

It is natural for a new Christian to want to know Jesus
better. The same desire should be experienced by every Christian. You consistently share with him your longing to discover
his thoughts and his desire. Amazingly, he becomes involved
in every intimate part of your life. Through being alone with
Jesus, you learn how to let him assume the full direction and
control of your life.

Spending time with God is one of the most important things

you will do in your Christian experience in preparation for witness. Before long you will cherish with joy every moment spent with him. For you the time will be an ever growing and thrilling relationship where love grows deeper and witness springs spontaneously from you to others.

Spiritual and personal development enable you to know God and to let him share with you. The time with him will be a normal and blessed time, an everyday experience which will lead you to a fresh, new relationship.

A good time to have this quiet time is in the early morning when you are fresh to begin a new day. You may prefer another time. Do your best to make it the same time every day, unhindered by the noises and pressures about you. Guard the time. God waits for you as you wait to be with him.

A specific place is important, especially one where you will be uninterrupted, for better communion with each other and where you can get away from distractions. Allow enough time to nourish and bless each moment. Ten minutes is a minimum. Fifteen is better.

Three things are important to this time: (1) reading God's Word (the Bible), (2) meditation, (3) prayer. These may be intermingled so that when you have finished the period both you and your thoughts will have the benefit of his blessings.

Study God's Word. Prepare your heart (Ps. 46:10). Open your heart and mind to God. His truths are especially prepared for you (Ps. 119:18). These become a guide for everyday experience.

Use the Bible. During the first period of your quiet time read carefully and thoughtfully. You may wish to take notes. Always think in terms of what God's Word means to you in your daily life. Do not hurry. Meditate and discover the great things God has in store for you as you read. Meditation makes God's Word a greater living reality as well as an exciting source of spiritual development and witness. Meditate thoughtfully upon your discoveries. At an early opportunity share and discuss your new insights with a friend.

Worship and prayer. Worship and prayer are the most meaningful areas of quiet time. Worship is prayer and prayer is worship. Prayer is conversing with God. Use conversational prayer. God reveals his desires for his children in worship and praise (Ps. 50:23). Praise him for being your creator and Savior. Simply say that you adore him, recognizing his majesty, greatness and sovereignty. Tell him you love him! Thanksgiving is essential in prayer. It is good to give thanks in all things (1 Thess. 5:18). When you pray be willing to admit frankly all your known sins (Ps. 66:18). Anything you have done wrong. Anything you thought which is unholy. Anything you have done against or to another person which is not good must be named specifically and laid before God. Call upon him to forgive and cleanse you from it (1 John 1:9). Then, having denounced the wrong, renounce it and forsake it. Determine that by God's help you will not again do this.

Ask God to continue to supply all your needs. Asking indicates better confidence with God. To ask is to exercise faith. Pray for others. Never be selfish in praying. If you intercede on behalf of others, you will develop a deeper love and concern for people. Pray for your family, friends, the church and its leaders, neighbors, government officials, missionaries and unsaved friends (Jas. 5:16).

While praying seek God's strength and leadership in sharing your faith every day with one who does not know Christ as you do. There are persons in your day-to-day experience whom God is preparing for your witness. Ask for sensitivity to bear their needs. By faith look for those persons.

Exercising these disciplines in a daily relationship with God will make you a more effective and efficient witness. You become victorious over evil. Your life bears the life-style of Jesus. From consistent life-living comes a consistent life-sharing.

It may be dangerous. You must understand that. Since Jesus gave his life to people, being with him may compel you to give your life to people. That means you get involved with people in the real issues of their existence.

A major second part of the equipping personal relationships is a discovery of the continuing and dwelling power of the Holy Spirit. Dr. E. Y. Mullin wrote in *Baptist Beliefs,* "It is a strange and significant fact that Christians for nearly two thousand years so generally neglected the New Testament as to the Holy Spirit. When interest suddenly revived in 1860–1900, God blessed the church with an amazing harvest. Evangelism becomes most effective when it depends on two mighty aspects of truths—the power of prayer and the work of the Holy Spirit."

A particularly good example is in Acts. The first seven chapters of Acts tell of the power of witness to Jerusalem. Acts 8–12 is a declaration of the witness under new power to Samaria. Acts 13–38 is a continuing expression of mighty witness to the Gentiles. None could actually take place without the outpouring of the Holy Spirit upon the believers.

They had a strong witness, bold, unashamed, and articulate. Their purpose for living was to tell what Jesus Christ had done for them. It was as Peter declared, "Whereof we are witnesses . . ." (Acts 2). This was his testimony and bold proclamation.

The power of the Holy Spirit moved them with an experience in Jesus Christ. The same is true for us today! If one wishes to become a mighty moving witness in evangelism the Holy Spirit must be in control of the believer's life. A person full of the Holy Spirit will be full of Christ, not full of himself. Others will be aware of the reality of the person involved in

Jesus Christ. In Acts 8:18 Simon Magus saw a difference in the Samaritans. He wanted that difference. He sought it.

Charles Spurgeon once declared, "We cannot promote the glory of God and bless the souls of men unless the Holy Spirit dwells in us in all his fullness." Truly, ordinary persons are made extraordinary persons. They are transformed and become transforming agents.

Evangelism in the power of the Holy Spirit has a new love. It is a love like Jesus Christ. Be with Christ in this relationship and a dynamic love is evident.

Paul wrote to the church at Philippi with an infectious joy. The entire letter was interspersed with terms as *rejoice, joy*. They reflected Jesus' own words, "That your joy may be full." To the church in Rome Paul wrote, "May the God of hope fill you with all joy and peace in believing, that you may abound in hope by the power of the Holy Spirit" (Rom. 15:13). An inevitable expression through the Holy Spirit is peace. Who can repute peace which passes all understanding? One fully yielded to Christ entreats peace in joyful witness.

With God a deep compassion becomes real. John Knox once cried, "Give me Scotland or I die." As Jesus observed the Samaritan villagers who followed a woman he had just conversed with at the well, he was overwhelmed with compassion. He sought to convey the same response to his disciples. The evidence of this compassion was proved when he died on the cross to save men from their sins. Those who have been saved from their sins in a new relationship through the power of his Holy One exercise the same compassion.

The Holy Spirit is the empowering weapon. He gives power to witness, power to convert. Jesus said, "You shall receive power. You shall be my witnesses, both in Jerusalem, in Samaria, and to the uttermost parts of the earth." The statement is clear to the believer. In the power of the Holy Spirit one may not feel like singing all the time but he feels like serving all the time. It is his witness. Witness in the power of the Holy Spirit, working in the life of the believer, opens their eyes that they may see, quickens their souls that they might experience, enpowers them to fulfill the will of the Father.

Professor Gaines Dobbins once said, "Evangelism is Christianity at work producing the fruits of discipleship. Evangelism is not the fighting of sporadic battles but an unceasing warfare. Evangelism is never defensive. It has but one strategy, *conquest.*" The strategy is "Christ in you, the hope of glory." Christ in you, the hope of glory, is the master working through you—the reality of the proclamation of the Good News. The effective witness is one who is with Jesus always sharing the Good News.

The unknown author of the book, *The Power-Full Christian,* tells of Sammy Morris, a young slave boy in the hinterland of West Africa who ran away because of brutal treatment and came to the coast where he saw another lad praying. He asked the lad what he was doing. The lad answered, "Talking to God." "Who is God?" asked the runaway boy. "He is my Father." "Then you are talking to your father." After this the young boy regarded God as his father. Though ignorant, unlettered and destitute in religious relationships, he developed a talking relationship to God that was both unusual and beautiful.

After a missionary described to him the wonderful joys of the Holy Spirit, he developed an intense longing to discover more. The missionary said, "If you want to know more you must go to Steven Merritt of New York. He taught me all I know of the Holy Spirit." The lad said, "I am going." Consequently, though the difficulties were pointed out clearly to him, Sammy Morris persuaded a blasphemous and brutal captain to let him work his passage on a sailing ship to America. Under these adverse circumstances the young lad had a quiet calm about the possibilities of his own new discoveries.

When he arrived in New York, he met Mr. Merritt and said, "I am Sammy Morris. I have just come from Africa to talk with you about the Holy Spirit." After a short conversation, Mr. Merritt took him to a mission and left him. Apparently, he was forgotten until approximately 10:30 P.M. when Merritt saw the lad surrounded by seventeen friends on their faces in prayer. Sammy had pointed *them* to Christ.

Observing their rejoicing relationship, Merritt said, "I had never seen such a sight. The Holy Spirit was in this figure of ebony, uncultured, uncouth, uncultivated African. Under the power of the Holy Spirit, his first night in America, he was winning souls for Immanuel—nearly a score."

Later Mr. Merritt took him in his coach to a funeral. On the way he began to point out different points of interest. As he was speaking of the great opera house, Sammy interrupted him to say, "Do you ever pray in the coach?" Merritt said, "Yes, very often." The lad placed his black hand upon Mr. Merritt and turned him around on his knees and said, "We will pray."

Merritt recalled, "He told the Holy Spirit that he had come from Africa to talk to me about God and I talked about everything else, when he was so anxious to hear and know about him. He asked God not to take out of my heart such things, and so fill me with himself that I would never preach, or write, or talk but of him, the Lord. Never have I known such a day. We were filled with the Holy Spirit."

When people heard about Sammy, many wrote for his photo. On seeing it for the first time Sammy exclaimed, "My picture is too ugly. Oh, that I could send them a picture of Jesus."

The amazing joy of this story is clear. Here was a lad filled with the power of the Holy Spirit. Spending so much time with him, he had a passion that would not die. He had a love which grew. Out of his experience he became a witness whose mark is left indelibly on the world.

Your equipment to evangelism is in your time with the Master, and your submission to the Lordship of Christ through the indwelling Holy Spirit.

12

Life-style Evangelism

Therefore, since we have so great a cloud of witnesses surrounding us, let us also lay aside every encumbrance, and the sin which so easily entangles us, and let us run with endurance the race that is set before us, fixing our eyes on Jesus, the author and perfecter of faith, who for the joy set before Him endured the cross, despising the shame, and has sat down at the right hand of the throne of God. For consider Him who has endured such hostility by sinners against Himself, so that you may not grow weary and lose heart. You have not yet resisted to the point of shedding blood, in your striving against sin; and you have forgotten the exhortation which is addressed to you as sons, "My son, do not regard lightly the discipline of the Lord, Nor faint when you are reproved by Him; For those whom the Lord loves He disciplines, And He scourges every son whom He receives" (Heb. 12:1–6).

12

Prologue

The first sermon I ever preached was in a jail. It was a mess. But everybody told me it was fine.

Occasionally I'd preach at church.

That winter, the first after I'd dedicated my life to the ministry, I went off to college. There I found even more opportunity to preach.

During this time a lot of the county schools were consolidating; people were leaving the farms and moving into the towns. Country churches were following the schools and the people into the towns. Old church buildings stood vacant all around.

Some of us at college felt these little churches should not be lost. We began going into these tiny communities and preaching in these old, abandoned church buildings. In about eight months we resurrected eleven churches and sixteen Sunday schools.

Jack Redford, a fellow minister and co-worker in our common journey, was my roommate. We bought an old car together and rattled around to these little churches. We were called "Bishop Hogue" and "Bishop Redford."

In one church we resurrected, I began preaching half-time. I did revivals many weekends.

I enjoyed evangelism. But I didn't feel called to be an evangelist or go into evangelism full-time.

And I had no real idea of "life-style evangelism." The

first time I ever used the term "life-style evangelism" was in an interview, just after I'd been elected director of the Evangelism Section of the Southern Baptist Home Mission Board.

I don't know where the words came from. The concept had been evolving in me for years out of my whole background and personal experiences. It was an attempt to impress upon people the realization that they witness by their lives.

Real evangelism is a life-giving, life-sharing experience. It is a commitment.

A person has to make a total commitment to Christ. Once he does, he commits himself to everything Christ is and stands for. He acts with sensitivity and understanding. That means giving a cup of cold water when someone needs it, but doing so "in Jesus' name."

Evangelism that becomes a person's life-style may be giving someone in need bread to eat, a house to live in, clothes to wear, because Christ said, "If you do it for the least of these, you do it for me."

By why do I do it?

That's what the guy who gets the bread or clothes or house is asking.

Does he know I'm a Christian? Not necessarily.

But he does if at the same time I give the bread or clothes or shelter I say, "I do this because I love you; I love you because Jesus loves you and I know Jesus' love." If I do it that way, then I know my witness is being fulfilled. I had discovered that there's more than a nominal Christian life. There's really more.

12

Life-style Evangelism

"It is high time," writes Seward Hiltner in *Ferment in Ministry*, "that we get evangelizing out of the theological basement. If we have a treasure to be shared with all men who will receive it, let us get on with it."

My thoughts have been to challenge you to "get on with it," to become involved in a walk upon this earth that can be described as "life-style evangelism"—that life-giving, life-sharing expression of one's faith that begins with the new-birth experience and ends with the last breath.

Living a moral life is no excuse for locked lips. Life through Christ speaks; it follows Jesus' example to act and to proclaim. It is evangelism as a style of life.

Life-style evangelism begins with an experience. A truly redeemed person has implanted within the reality that Jesus Christ is Savior, and that, without doubt, God in Christ "reconciled the world to himself."

The life-style evangelism experience helps a person realize who he is: a sinner in need of the grace of God. And who God is: the father who gave his fullest revelation in his Son, Jesus, the hope of humankind. Writes E. G. Homerighausen in *Evangelism,* "That [revelation] is a mandate announcing

God has visited us; has assumed full responsibility for us; has identified himself with us so that nothing can separate us from his love; has borne our tragic lot and tragic perversity; has tasted our despair and death; has won a decisive victory over the powers of evil; has opened up heavenly possibilities through the resurrection and the power of the Spirit."

After the Holy Spirit begins his work, life-style evangelism develops as the Christian matures. Said Jesus, "Learn of me." Paul wrote, "Grow up, go beyond the milk, eat the meat." One problem in many churches is the large number of immature Christians who never get beyond the superficial aspects of their church membership into the gut-deep demands of the gospel life. No wonder our churches constantly find themselves in trouble. No wonder the world does not follow the "Christian example."

The world's people want a fresh awareness of the grandeur and glory of the Good News of Jesus Christ. They don't find it among immature Christians who treat their faith as something fragile or unreal, as if it would not withstand logical reasoning or probing examination, or as if it were a Sunday-only sermon without basis for daily expression.

Empty and shallow conversion will not do. Hypocrisy will not do. The twentieth century demands Christians exhibit a maturing relationship with God. A relationship which is honest, real, consistently exploring the depths and demands of faith—despite personal frailties—will win the respect, at least, of a world filled with deceit, despair, defeat.

The Christian life is a process, not a plan—an enveloping, growing, disciplining, searching, continuous struggle toward the perfect example of Christ's thirty-three years. It demands action—sharing Christ's promise physically and verbally.

"Every man and woman has the right to hear what a fellow human being believes to be the way of salvation from emptiness and meaninglessness," says George Sweazy in *Effective*

Evangelism. "In the emerging new age every man has not only the right but the responsibility to speak."

Life-style evangelism stands as the missing link between the heart of God and the heart of humankind. Life-style evangelism calls for a one-way commitment that recognizes the hopeless condition of people today and the direction that God gives.

The New Testament account of the lives of Peter and John illustrates what happens when evangelism becomes an individual's style of life. From their three-year companionship with Jesus, the two men developed into mature disciples. At Pentecost, the outpouring of the Holy Spirit filled them. Overwhelmed by compassion for the world, they witnessed Jesus; they proclaimed him naturally; they boldly declared that he was the Messiah, the everlasting fulfillment of history. Whatever they did, whatever they said, was said or done in the name of Jesus. They did not witness of a church, an organization, or themselves. Peter and John simply conducted themselves as representatives of the truth that in Jesus Christ the kingdom of God had broken in history. A new beginning had been made in life and a process had begun which one day would consume the entire universe.

These early Christians were living proof that the life, death, and resurrection of Jesus had radically affected their lives. The conversion experience had been real; they were "new people."

John said, "We can only tell you what we have seen, have heard, and have felt, and we know to be right."

In a south central Oklahoma community so small the grocery store and gasoline station are combined, the Baptist church has come alive. Its young pastor was turned on to Christ, and his infectious enthusiasm spread through the congregation. With new joy pervading the fellowship, attendance doubled. One Wednesday night a young woman came to the services. During a period of sharing, the pastor asked if she would like to tell what God had done for her. Looking uncomfortable and defiant, she said, "Nothing." Instead of replying in a kind manner, the church members lovingly began to explain how God moved in their lives. The young woman went home with a new outlook. Later that night she listed the things God had done for her. In this experience she found salvation. The next morning when the owner came to open his grocery-gas station, the young woman was waiting at the door.

"Can I help you?" the man asked.

"Yes," she said simply. "I would like to place this sheet of paper on your door or window."

She handed her list to the owner, who read it, tears gathering in his eyes. Finally, he said, "I'm glad you want to do that, and of course I'll let you. But why do you feel it's necessary?"

"Because I want everyone to know I was wrong last night," the woman replied, "and since I can't see everyone personally, I think this is the best place to tell them. A lot of people in the community come here, and they'll read my list and know what God has done for me."

A bold church reflecting the joy of its experience in Christ had reached out to one in need, and the church's boldness gave courage to this young woman. And both the church's action and the woman's reaction became natural consequences of being filled with the Holy Spirit.

A. T. Pierson has said, "Witnessing is a necessity of a truly redeemed soul. A light that does not shine, a spring that does not flow, a seed that does not grow is no more an anomaly than a life in Christ that does not witness for Christ." Like Christ's early followers, today's disciples must be as sensitive to the leadership of the Holy Spirit as they are sensitive to the needs of people with whom they come into day-to-day contact. They must carry the Word in their hearts and evidence it in their lives; they must feel their responsibility to share it without prejudice or fear. Today's disciples must be consistent witnesses.

In today's world they are revolutionaries who discover witnessing is a way of life, not a duty to be performed.

Scores of opportunities await us, for God's intent is for his followers to share today, everyday, their Good News, not as forced witnesses, but merely because they believe Jesus' commission. In doing so, they become life-style evangelists—men and women moving from the initial new-birth experience through the constant maturation of Bible study and Christian thought into a pattern of existence that equates breathing with doing the will of God among the lost people of the world.

Perhaps the prayer of martyred missionary Jim Elliott best expresses what life-style evangelism is all about. Elliott wrote in his Bible:

> God deliver me from the dread asbestos of other things, saturate me with the oil of thy Spirit that I may be a flame . . . Father, take my life, yea, my blood if thou wilt, and consume it with thy enveloping fire. I would not save it for it is not mine to save; have it, Lord, have it all. Pour out my life as an oblation for the world. Make me thy fuel, O flame of God.

Epilogue

Good News is hope! We live by hope—hope for what God is doing now, hope for what he will do in the future. Today there is Good News! Good news that God loves all men.

Such news, says Jesus, will be forever redeeming, transforming, and making disciples of men. What a difference God can make in the world of men's circumstances. Jesus did it for the woman at the well and for the blind man named Bartimaeus. He did it for Lazarus.

It is Good News that the promise of the kingdom of heaven is near. What Good News! God is in Christ reconciling the world to himself. This is news that can be told. We are responsible to obediently share that message. We must be motivated by a fresh awareness of the grandeur and the glory of this gospel of Jesus Christ.

For the church to survive today, this Good News must be proclaimed. It is our hope and the work of it is evangelism. Evangelism proclaims the Good News. Evangelism shares it on a one-to-one basis. Evangelism believes every person is a sacred possibility for the presence of the power of God in Christ. Eternal issues are now at stake.

Evangelism is not seasonal. Careful preparation may be helpful. Evangelism must be done at all times and everywhere. It depends upon enlistment of the manpower of the church and every member in it must be God-centered. The early believers took the gospel everywhere. They believed Jesus Christ to be the Lord. To them he was ultimate authority in heaven and in earth. No doubt, he was the Lord of the nations and his spirit was at work in all history. They were confident his ministry would be consummated at the end of the age. So, Paul said to

Timothy, *"Do the work of an evangelist." Never did he say, "Now, Timothy, you should call a meeting about the matter of evangelism." No, he said, "Do it!"*

Evangelism, our hope in spreading the Good News, depends on the dynamics of the Holy Spirit. No human personality nor organization with its trappings will suffice. The Lordship of Christ is evidently the basis of it.

The New Testament believers set us an example. They had a grand and glorious character about the practice of it. This is what motivated them in spite of their frailties and weaknesses. They believed the action in Jesus Christ was crucial for the life of man and nations. It was news of unprecedented action.

They believed what Jesus Christ started would continue to the end of the age. Their apostolic zeal was motivated by the future hope—a hope that was already at work in them and the world. They learned from Jesus that he did not come to restore the past but to fulfill it.

For us to remain alive in the ministry of reconciliation we must maintain the center of our church life through evangelism. If we fail we perish. If we fail, our failure lies somewhere in our unwillingness to make evangelism the priority God set for the church and for the need of the world.

When a person is called to be a follower of Christ, he is also called to be a witness. Samuel Escobar said, "We might choose to be silent witnesses, but if our life is really transforming by God's Spirit, sooner or later we will be called to give an account of our hope. . . . In the face of difficulties and hardships the command of Christ cannot be changed: 'You will be my witnesses.'"

I have written this book out of the conviction that God has given such a commission. It may have appeared to be staggering, the responsibility overwhelming, but when I have listened to God and watched him at work, I discovered what Paul had said, "The love of Christ leaves us no choice" (2 Cor. 5:14, NEB).

Bibliography

Bader, Jesse M. *Evangelism in a Changing World.* The Bethany Press, 1957.

Boer, Harry R. *Pentecost and Missions.* Wm. B. Eerdmans Publishing Co., 1961.

Hiltner, Seward. *Ferment in Ministry,* Abingdon Press, 1969.

Leavell, R. Q. *Evangelism: Christ's Imperative Commission.* Broadman Press, 1951.

Stott, John R. W. *Our Guilty Silence.* Inter-Varsity Press, 1967.

Smart, James D. *Rebirth of the Ministry.* Westminster Press, 1960.

Sweazy, George E. *Effective Evangelism.* Harper & Row, 1953.

Trueblood, Elton. *The Company of the Committed.* Harper & Brothers, 1961.

DATE DUE

AP 19 '70			
OC 26 '83			
DE 2 1 '85			
GAYLORD			PRINTED IN U.S.A.